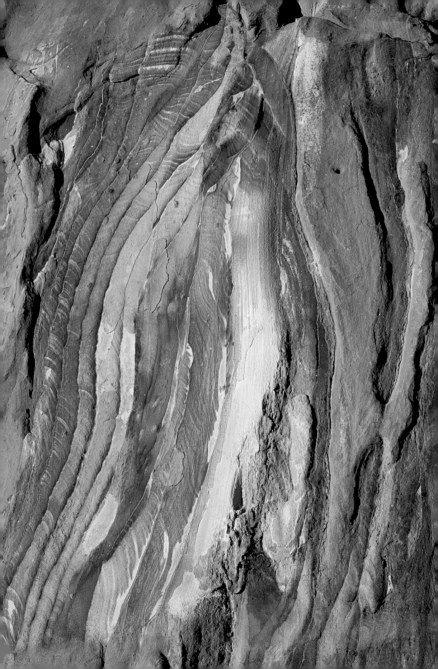

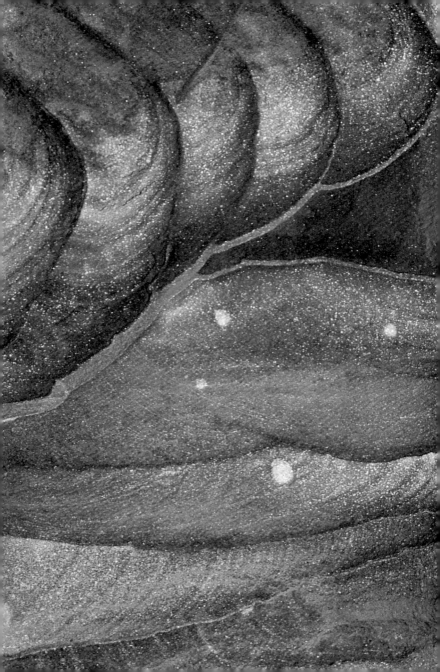

CONTENTS

PETRA
THE ROSE-RED CITY

Christian Augé and Jean-Marie Dentzer

 **Thames & Hudson**

"Despite the appalling state into which it has fallen under the Empire of the Crescent [the Ottoman Empire], Petra still remains the eighth wonder of the world! Those unable to visit it dream of it; those who, like us, have gone there wish to see it again and study it further. After centuries of silence, it has returned to life, and has become the object of scientific expeditions, full of fascination."

Adélaïde Sargenton-Galichon,
Sinaï, Maân, Pétra: Sur les traces d'Israël et chez les Nabatéens
(*Sinai, Ma'an, Petra: On the Trail of Israel and the Land of the Nabataeans*), 1904

CHAPTER 1
PETRA REVEALED

Left: El Khazneh, Petra's best-known monument, is depicted here by David Roberts (c. 1839). The tomb is almost certainly that of a king or queen. While its date remains open to dispute, the composite architecture, influenced by the art of Alexandria, suggests the 1st century BC. Right: another image by Roberts shows Beduins of the period.

Clandestine expeditions

On August 22, 1812, a Swiss traveler—the first European in centuries—looked in amazement upon the tall, rose-colored stone facade of the mausoleum called El Khazneh, the so-called Treasury of the Pharaoh. He had found the hidden city of Petra, which leaps suddenly to the eye of the visitor who emerges into its sheltered valley, after a half-hour trek through the narrow defile called the Siq.

Disguised in Arab garb and using the name Sheikh Ibrahim, the explorer Johann Ludwig Burckhardt (1784–1817) had crossed the lands of the Mideast, making his way from Damascus to Egypt and traversing what is now the nation of Jordan. At the time, it was not easy for non-Muslims to travel in this troubled region of the Ottoman Empire, and too pointed an interest in antiquities was suspect, for they were deemed the work of infidels. But Burckhardt had heard that extraordinary relics were hidden within a strange natural fortress near the valley of Wadi Musa, whose name means the "Stream of Moses." He therefore presented himself as a pilgrim who wished to sacrifice a goat at the

Below: Burckhardt dressed as "Sheikh Ibrahim." When he visited Petra, the political and religious situation in the region was tense. He was careful to keep his curiosity from arousing the distrust of his guide and the hostility of the residents. He described El Khazneh—"one of the most elegant ruins of antiquity existing in Syria"—in great detail, but saw the temple of Qasr al-Bint only briefly. Left: unable to make sketches, he retained only a superficial memory of the tombs, as evidenced by this poor sketch, done later. His recollection was clearly colored by sites in Egypt: "Their shape," he wrote erroneously, "is most often that of a truncated pyramid."

tomb of the prophet Hārūn (Aaron), visible beyond these ruins, atop a nearby mountain peak. Thus he first came upon one of the world's most beautiful ancient places.

Closely watched by his guide, Burckhardt had to content himself with a quick visit through the city, and was unable to take accurate

W illiam John Bankes was living in Egypt, drawing ancient monuments, when he learned of Burckhardt's discovery. Having considerable means and a taste for archaeology, he gathered a team for an expedition to Petra, including the guide-interpreter Giovanni Finati and two British naval officers, Charles Leonard Irby and James Mangles. But rivalries among tribal chiefs in the area forced them to cut short their stay, and they published only summary reports of their trip. These appeared in London in 1823, at the same time as the posthumous work of Burckhardt. Nonetheless, the visit was important for the number of new ruins discovered, including the so-called Turkmaniyya Tomb, with its Nabataean inscription. Left: in this watercolor of El Khazneh, glimpsed between cliffs, Bankes attempts to render the effect that strikes the visitor upon emerging from the narrow rock cleft called the Siq. This was the dramatic point of view later adopted by generations of photographers.

notes or sketch its many monuments. But what he saw convinced him of the importance of the site. Remarkably, he identified it swiftly. "In comparing the evidence of several [classical] authors," he wrote, "it seems very likely that the ruins of Wadi Musa are those of ancient Petra."

His news soon spread among the Europeans who had settled throughout the Levant and Egypt. Muhammad 'Alī Pasha, viceroy of Egypt, was then beginning to modernize his country by welcoming Western scholars and technicians. In fact, researchers had long been speculating about the location of the ancient capital of a mysterious people called the Nabataeans, mentioned in certain ancient texts.

The local tribes were hostile to strangers; nevertheless, other Europeans soon sought to explore Petra. In May

1818, a group of some ten people traveled there from Jerusalem, among them an Englishman named William John Bankes, who spent two busy days on the site, making drawings. The visitors climbed Jabal Hārūn, the mountain of Aaron (now called Mount Hor), which rises above the site; from there, through a telescope, they saw the facade of ad-Deir, the so-called Monastery Tomb, crowning another peak. They crossed the ruined city and described its principal monuments in an account of their trip published in 1823. To this day, however, Bankes's sketches remain largely unpublished.

B elow: El Khazneh in a watercolor by Bankes. The column fragment to the left of the tomb entry has been restored. In the past, the Wadi Musa stream flowed though the Siq, bordered by oleanders. To avoid

The first archaeological missions

More fruitful was the visit undertaken in 1828 by two Frenchmen, Léon de Laborde (1807–69) and Louis-Maurice Linant de Bellefonds (1799–1883). Linant had been exploring Egypt and Sudan for a decade and was familiar with the Sinai Peninsula. The young Laborde joined him after a long period of traveling in Turkey and Syria. Leaving Cairo, their caravan, "fifteen camels and eighteen people" strong, traveled along the Wadi Araba (a *wadi* is a valley) to Petra. Toward the end of March they made camp amid its ruins. In Wadi Musa a plague was raging; still, despite the fears of their guides, they stayed for six days, taking painstaking notes and measurements and above all making innumerable drawings. "We did not only want to see Petra," wrote Laborde, "we wanted, as our Arabs said, to take it away in portfolios." They visited the entire ancient city, the principal ravines within and around it, and the narrow aisle of the Siq, sketching most of the great tombs, climbing ad-Deir, and recording enough particulars to draw the first map

sudden dangerous floods, such as occurred in 1963, its course was later diverted before the entry to the narrow passage.

of Petra. On the return journey, they also described
Sabra, one of the most picturesque sites in the vicinity.

Their expedition, the first true archaeological mission,
marked a considerable advance in the volume and
precision of information gathered. Upon returning to
Europe, Laborde presented his findings in a publication

A drawing by Laborde of the outer Siq, beyond El Khazneh. The top of the facade of this tomb, which bore a Greek epitaph, collapsed in 1847.

that was at once glossy and scholarly. His *Voyage de l'Arabie Pétrée* (*Voyage to Arabia Petraea*), rich in illustrations, introduced Petra and its founders, the Nabataeans, to the Western public.

A mysterious kingdom

To these first travelers, nurtured on biblical and classical references, the name Petra did not mean much. It is mentioned rarely and only in passing by a few Greek and Roman authors. Just two texts discuss it more thoroughly: the *Library of History* of Diodorus of Sicily (90–20 BC) and the *Geography* by the geographer and historian Strabo (c. 64/63 BC–after AD 23), contemporaries, respectively, of Julius Caesar and the emperor Augustus. Both describe it as the capital of the Nabataeans, a people made wealthy by the caravan trade, who Diodorus says were in the region by 312 BC, shortly after the death of Alexander the Great. Writing from a distance of three centuries, the Roman authors presented two contradictory pictures of this folk: first, that they were autonomous nomads, and second, that they were settled peasants, dwelling comfortably in a luxurious city.

The Nabataean kingdom was extensive and powerful in the area, but its independence ended when it was annexed in AD 106 by Rome. In the reign of the emperor Trajan, Petra became one of the principal cities of the Roman province of Arabia Petraea (comprising Jordan, south Syria, the Sinai, and parts of Israel and Saudi Arabia). The Nabataeans themselves fell into oblivion.

Above: Léon de Laborde, dressed as a Beduin; above left: his finely rendered drawing of the interior of the building called the Soldier's Triclinium at Wadi Farasa in Petra. (In the distance can be seen a related tomb, said to be that of a Roman soldier.)

The rediscovery of their capital in the 19th century restored their name and place in the historical record.

The nature of the information Laborde gathered on the Nabataeans was characteristic of his period. Like other 19th-century antiquarians, he had studied the principal relevant passages in the ancient writers, but he also considered the Old Testament an indispensable source. The Nabataeans are not mentioned there—for good reason, since they settled in the region long after the events that it recounts. In that era, this had been the country of the Edomites, descendants of Esau, whom the Bible presents as opposing the passage of the Jews through their land during the Exodus. They aroused the interest of researchers in history, geography, and biblical studies, disciplines that were experiencing a great renaissance at the beginning of the 19th century. Eager to identify the route and stopping points of the Exodus, Laborde and others noticed that many local Arabic names were biblical: the "Stream of Moses," and the "Treasury of the Pharaoh," for example.

B elow: the great tombs carved into the cliffs of the Khubtha mountain, identified by their modern names. They are, from right: the Urn Tomb, the Silk Tomb, the Corinthian Tomb, and the Palace Tomb. The drawing is by Louis-Maurice Linant de Bellefonds, who stood by the stream, with his back to the theater. To save time in drawing, Laborde and Linant divided the viewpoints for each monument between them.

The Nabataean myth

Laborde's book received a favorable response in the
scholarly world, and the quality of its engravings stirred
a general interest in the Nabataeans that quickly became
a popular craze. The public's imagination fed on what

Above: the Palace
Tomb and the
Corinthian Tomb in an
1845–48 watercolor by the
Englishman William
Bartlett.

Laborde's sumptuous folio, with pictures and commentary, appeared between 1830 and 1833. "One must not judge this monument by its present state," he wrote of the Palace Tomb. "It must once have been much taller. A great line [frieze] completed these three tiers of columns, giving the whole a unity that perhaps compensated for the proportional flaws and the irregularity of its different parts." This sepulcher, probably that of a member of the nobility, has the largest rock-hewn facade in Petra: 161 feet wide by 151 feet tall (49 by 46 meters). Its uppermost level had been partially built up above the cliff with masonry faced with a cladding that no longer exists, but that Laborde observed and described. He was not very enthusiastic about the nearby Corinthian Tomb, which he deemed "a bad imitation of El Khazneh."

Laborde called the "vague traditions" surrounding the site and on the mystery that shrouded the origins of its people. Where had they come from? When had they first arrived? Why did they vanish? Even today these questions linger. The Nabataeans had flourished and faded in an Arab land, and this was a period of passionate interest in Orientalism

L eft: at a height of 52½ feet (16 meters), the imposing arch that once spanned the entry to the Bab el-Siq, or aisle of the Siq, is captured in a lithograph by David Roberts. It collapsed in 1896, leaving only a few traces in the walls and some niches with moldings. The narrow passage, which is quite steep at this point, constituted the principal point of access to the city and was very easy to defend. Modern archaeology and historiography rely a great deal on the notes and precise drawings of the first travelers, who saw the monuments when they were in a better state than they are today, and documented some ruins that no longer exist.

J.L. Gérome, H. de Barthel

and all things Arabian. It was not surprising that a degree of exaggeration crept into accounts of them.

By the 1830s, Petra was a prime destination for travelers, who often visited it in conjunction with a trip to the Sinai or other holy places. In the Levant, as in Egypt, expeditions were risky, as disputes among local tribes were common. Most tours were organized by *drogmans,* who were at once interpreters, guides, and factotums, and whose name has been anglicized as dragomans. Such excursions were quite expensive, as it was necessary to make arrangements through a multitude of intermediaries, and local chiefs did their best to earn the maximum profit.

Scholars, adventurers, and simple tourists followed one another to Petra. Their accounts, sometimes written with talent, readily took up the literary themes of the day: the proximity of the theater to the tombs, for example, suggested the nearness of pleasure to death; the drama of a lost civilization, troubling the serenity of the desert, was also popular. The sudden discovery of this dead city, hidden in the hollows of the rocks, and the vision of its strange, ornate architecture integrated with untamed nature, excited the enthusiasm of a culture steeped in Romanticism. Speculation and exotic tales about Petra and its people flourished. And thus was born a powerful myth that persists to this day.

The true discovery of the Nabataeans

In the 19th century, scholarly research remained an individual endeavor that often endured for many decades. Enlightened amateur archaeologists and scholars of all

B elow: by 1868, Petra had become a major destination of cultural and artistic tourism. In that year a caravan of French painters traveled to the Fayum, the Sinai, and Petra. It included Jean-Léon Gérôme, Léon Bonnat, Paul Lenoir, the *drogman* Joseph Moussali, and the photographer Albert Goupil. They required no less than twenty-seven camels to transport all their equipment! The atmosphere was merry but the overall picture of Petra was disappointing. As Lenoir recounts, "two days of torrential rains relegated us to utter inactivity; these hours were pleasantly spent in inventing Franco-Greek

...at, E. Journault, W Tertas, P. Lenoir, Joseph Moussaly, A. Goupil, R. Goubie
l'expédition en Orient. 1868.
Akabah. 19 Mars.

inscriptions about those tombs that were most meaningful to the eye and to the minds…of lovers of illustrated puzzles."

A verse by the British poet John William Burgon, written in 1840, established the romantic fame of Petra; it was for evermore a "rose-red city half as old as time." Like many other writers of the period fascinated by the place, Burgon never went to Petra, but dreamed of it through published pictures. Especially compelling were the watercolors of a Scottish painter, David Roberts, who had accompanied the businessman John Kinnear to the site in 1839. Between 1842 and 1849, these were copied in colored lithographs and collected in an attractive book entitled *Egypt, Syria, and the Holy Land*. Roberts had been tempted to undertake his journey by the engravings of Linant de Bellefonds and Laborde. Far left: his view of the theater with the opening of the Outer Siq and the Wadi Musa; near left: the necropolis. Roberts exaggerated the heights to create a Romantic effect.

nationalities were among the visitors who reached Petra. Their interests were diverse: there were specialists in biblical studies, such as the American theologian Edward Robinson, who went in 1838; Assyriologists, such as the English archaeologist Austen Henry Layard, who went in 1840; and the geographers Gotthilf H. von Schubert and Jules de Bertou, who made the important discovery in 1837 that the level of the Dead Sea is far below that of the Mediterranean. In 1864, the expedition of the renowned archaeologist and Orientalist Honoré d'Albert, Duc de Luynes, inaugurated research of a greater scientific accuracy. His detailed report included an inventory of the entire site. Nonetheless, the rock-hewn tombs, the most arresting buildings, continued to attract more interest than the less spectacular remains of the ancient city.

Language, inscriptions, coins

At this point, other avenues of research opened up. Specialists in Semitic languages became interested in Nabataean epigraphy, building their first studies upon the numerous copies of inscriptions brought back by earlier travelers. In 1840, Eduard Beer identified the Nabataean alphabet (a semicursive that may have some connection with later Arabic script), and the language was recognized as a form of western Aramaic. In the 1850s, the French epigraphists Melchior de Vogüé and William Henry Waddington did fieldwork on writing in southern Syria. In the Sinai, ancient pilgrim graffiti were also plentiful. Meanwhile, French and German linguists tackled the question of the lost language's structure. This dual effort, the systematic gathering of inscriptions and linguistic

Above: these Nabataean inscriptions were uncovered in Petra by Julius Euting, a German epigraphist working at the end of the 19th century and the beginning of the 20th. Below: inscriptions from Shaubak, to the north of the city. The epigraphic record includes thousands of inscriptions, some of them sketchy, carved in all sorts of stone. Those from the Sinai, notably from Wadi Mokatteb, the "Valley of Writing," had intrigued pilgrims and travelers since antiquity, and had sometimes been attributed to the Jews of the Exodus. Orientalists soon became interested in them. When Eduard Beer worked on the Nabataean script in 1840, these graffiti were recognized as Nabataean.

research, has continued ever since. Around the same time, numismatists began collecting and identifying silver and bronze coins issued by Nabataean kings in the two centuries before the Roman conquest. Archaeologists were soon able to decipher the names and titles of kings and queens that they bore. Once these were properly classified (after numerous revisions), historians were able to establish a sequence of those sovereigns considered to be the most important.

Thus, more than the exploration of Petra itself, linguistic, epigraphic, and numismatic studies gradually permitted the construction of a political and dynastic history of the Nabataeans, as well as providing some information about their religion. The debate about the

Nabataean commemorative citations are common and yield numerous personal names. A great number begin with *Shlm*, "Peace!" Many date from the 2d and 3d centuries AD, and some include Christian symbols, such as the cross visible below, that may have been added at a later time. The animal figures were added by the Beduins, who have always etched such images into the rocks. Invocations and dedications naming the divinities and their followers are frequent at Petra. They are sometimes accompanied by sketches of a cult object called a baetyl, depicted here (above left) as a rectangle with squared eyes, a horned altar (above), and hand- or footprints indicating the sacred nature of the place.

origin of this people was not resolved, but rather fueled by new knowledge. They seem to have come from the Arabian peninsula, but it is difficult to pinpoint just when they settled in the land of Edom.

A considerably broadened view of the Nabataean world emerges from all these efforts: it comprised the

In 1876, Charles Doughty (1843–1926) joined a caravan to Mecca and traveled across the Hejaz. Below: he brought back sketches of the immense facades of the rock-hewn tombs of Hegra. Although the same architectural character-istics are found in a

regions of Petra, the Sinai, and the Negev and extended to the massif of the Hauran in southern Syria and a large part of the Hejaz, in present-day Saudi Arabia. Between 1875 and 1877, the Englishman Charles M. Doughty discovered the southern Nabataean city of Hegra at Medain Saleh in the Hejaz, while German and French epigraphists in the last quarter of the 19th century and the beginning of the 20th found many inscriptions in this region.

series of tombs in Petra, the great inscriptions at Hegra, often bearing specific dates, provide better chronological signposts than those in the capital city.

First work on the site

In the years before World War I, the Ottoman Empire grew more accessible to Westerners, and research at Petra benefited from a somewhat calmer political situation. From this point on, exploration was directed by large organizations, especially European and American univer-sities and centers located in the Middle East, such as the Ecole Biblique et Archéologique Française, the French school of archaeology and biblical studies in Jerusalem.

Local residents in the area continued to be inhos-pitable and, strictly speaking, prohibited excavations. Nevertheless, visitors to Petra had progressively more precise objectives, which for the most part they were able to accomplish. For example, specialists from the French

Right: in 1896, Dominican monks from the Ecole Biblique et Archéologique Française de Jerusalem made a squeeze impres-sion of the monumental inscription of the Turkmaniyya Tomb. This text, engraved some 20 feet (6 meters) from the ground, confirms the sacred and inalienable nature of the tomb. The richness of its technical vocabulary lends it considerable linguistic interest.

Ecole Biblique methodically copied all the inscriptions on the many monuments, and the German Heinrich Kohl studied the temple at Qasr al-Bint. Investigations extended to several other sites in the Nabataean region, including the Hejaz, which was surveyed by two French clerics, Father Antonin Jaussen and Father Raphaël Savignac, from 1907 to 1910. They presented their documentation in volumes entitled *Mission archéologique en Arabie* (*Archaeological Expeditions in Arabia,* 1909, 1914). All in all, this was an era of great undertakings that culminated in publications of the first significance.

The Czech Aloïs Musil had traversed the Nabataean region before 1896 as far as the Syrian-Mesopotamian desert and the middle of the Arabian peninsula, and described Petra in detail, particularly studying its

Scholars, in particular the Germans, conducted extensive documentary photographic projects at the beginning of the 20th century. These were made possible by advances in optics, and were supplemented by drawings. In this way, the monuments, each duly numbered, were recorded on detailed maps. Below: the necropolis to the south of the theater, in a sketch taken from Brünnow and von Domaszewski's *Die*

ethnology. But his book *Arabia Petraea,* which appeared in 1907–8, was soon outstripped by the nearly complete inventory of the religious monuments of Petra that Gustaf Dalman, a German researcher, drew up between 1908 and 1912, as well as the treatise of Rudolf Ernst Brünnow and Alfred von Domaszewski, *Die Provincia Arabia* (*The Arabian Province*), published between 1904 and 1909 in collaboration with the epigraphist Julius Euting. In 1904–5, Brünnow and von Domaszewski led numerous expeditions to Petra, central Jordan, the ancient land of Moab, and the Hauran. All visible ruins were sketched

Provincia Arabia, which listed 851 separate items, ranging from simple graffiti to the most important buildings in Petra.

The British archae-ologist Alexander Kennedy poses here in the interior of a great tomb, which shows numerous *loculi* (indi-vidual vaults) carved into the sandstone wall. From the end of the 19th century, photography played an essential role in archaeological research at Petra, especially when the methodical excavations of monuments began.

and located on maps, inventories were taken, and many items were photographed. This documentation process was invaluable, and continues to be used today.

World War I interrupted research only to a degree. In fact, as English troops advanced through the Mideast, the Turkish authorities charged three Germans, Thomas Wiegand, Wilhelm Bachmann, and Carl Watzinger, with protecting the monuments of Petra. For the first time, the Ottoman government acknowledged the importance of the city and its architecture.

Thus, a wide-ranging, multi-disciplinary study of the civilization of Nabataea began with a narrow branch of biblical archaeology. Before the war, Dalman made the first serious attempts at historical synthesis. After the war, the territory then called Transjordan was placed under a British mandate, and the English scholar Sir Alexander Kennedy was able to include the Royal Air Force's remarkable photographs, including early aerial views, in a popular 1925 book, *Petra: Its History and Monuments.*

A staircase makes it possible to climb up to the urn atop ad-Deir. It is 30 feet (9 meters) tall, an indication of the great size of the whole monument.

Modern excavations and archaeological projects

In 1929, a comprehensive study by Albert Kammerer, *Pétra et la Nabatène* (*Petra and Nabataea*), was published in France. That same year, two British archaeologists, George Horsfield and Agnes Conway, undertook the first strictly scientific excavations in a residential sector of the city. In the years before World War II, many other buildings and important tombs, including El Khazneh, were excavated by the British and American archaeologists J. C. Ellis, Margaret Murray, and W. F. Albright. Projects were carried out at many other Nabataean sites, particularly Wadi Rum and Khirbet Tannur.

In 1946, Transjordania became the independent Hashemite Kingdom of Jordan; archaeological activities came under the administration of its Department of Antiquities. In 1954, major preservation and excavation projects were undertaken. The first stages of these concentrated on the important monuments clustered in the center of the city. Their purpose was to clarify the chronology of the buildings and to fill in missing information regarding the period in which Nabataea was transformed from a nomadic into a settled culture.

In this satellite photograph of Petra, the deep course of the Wadi Musa and the lower city within its ring of jagged peaks are readily distinguishable. Recent aerial and satellite photography, much of it by the French National Institute of Geography, makes an exact mapping of the region possible. These photos enable researchers to understand the environment of the site, its geographical peculiarities, and the problems of contemporary land development.

A more complex view of the Nabataeans

Since mid-century, research has been continuous and intensive. The dig itself still barely scratches the surface of the site. So far, the great monuments, houses, and workshops have been revealed. Also of interest are a network of roads and a complex hydraulic system for the collecting and conveying of water. Archaeologists are also studying the agricultural record of the surrounding area.

Thanks to scientific methods now available to archaeologists, the daily life of the Nabataeans is slowly being uncovered. Aerial and satellite photography have assisted in the drafting of precise maps. Current work has now entered a phase of inventory taking reminiscent of that conducted at the beginning of the century.

Such techniques have also been employed in other areas of the ancient Nabataean realm in Jordan, the Negev, the Sinai, the Hejaz, and southern Syria. The analysis of artisanal work—ceramics, statuettes of bronze or terra-cotta, and coins—has become more refined, using such methods as close comparison among many examples. Gradually, scholars are building a better understanding of Nabataean sculpture, architecture, and other arts. Little by little, typology and chronology have

On the left wall of the Siq (seen here at right), just before El Khazneh, some great sculptures carved directly into the sandstone were very recently uncovered. Unfortunately rather incomplete, they depict over-life-size camel herders dressed in long robes, heading with their beasts into the ancient city. The beasts' feet, which would have been at ground level, are no longer visible. These statues, located near cult niches, may have been *ex-voto* offerings by either the residents of Petra or pilgrims. They remind us of the importance of camels in the economy and life of the Nabataeans.

become clearer. The study of the language owes a great
deal to the work of the Abbé Jean Starcky, the author in
1966 of a remarkable cross-disciplinary summary study
on Petra, the Nabataeans, and their religion.
Recently, linguistic researchers have turned
to Egyptian and other papyri, in addition
to the inscriptions themselves, examining
connections with neighboring languages
and drawing comparisons. A more

complex and nuanced view of the
Nabataeans emerges, in which it is clear
that their society did not end with the
Roman conquest.

Such rapid progress would not have
been possible without the amicable,
international collaboration of the
numerous expeditions that have met
in Petra. These have been welcomed
by the Jordanian Department
of Antiquities and Jordanian
specialists such as Dr. Fawzi
Zayadine, whose interest in the
Nabataeans is passionate. These
research programs must take
into consideration the
management and preservation

Above left: a Jordanian
archaeological team
clears rubble from the
Siq. A recent project is
studying the ancient
paving, large areas of
which are well-preserved,
as well as the system of
channels that supplied
the city with water.

Left: the ez-Zantur hill is one of the few sectors of Petra to have undergone methodical excavation. Since 1988, archaeologists from the University of Basel working there have brought to light an important complex of houses from both the Nabataean and Roman periods.

Far left: recently found by Beduins in Wadi Mataha, this statue of Artemis-Diana, the Greco-Roman goddess of the hunt, stands 3.9 feet (1.2 meters) tall. It is the most important bronze work of art found in Jordan. The goddess is depicted running, and probably once carried a bow, as she does on imperial-era coins from Jerash, the city of which she was patron. It is a fine example of the classically influenced metal sculptures that adorned Roman cities of the Eastern Empire in the 2d and 3d centuries AD, few of which survive.

of a site that covers almost 50 square miles (80 square kilometers), visited by ever-increasing crowds of tourists. Since 1985, Petra has been on the UNESCO list of world-heritage sites.

Archaeology there must be carried out with sensitivity to its fragility. Studies and planning must take a regional perspective that incorporates data on the geomorphology and climate of the region. In this way, we will acquire a better grasp of living conditions in the ancient city, and of the populace's exploitation of natural resources over a period of some 2,500 years. Only thus will we be able to insert the mysterious Nabataeans seamlessly into the historical continuum.

"They live in the open air, claiming as native land a wilderness that has neither rivers nor abundant springs… It is their custom neither to plant grain, set out any fruit-bearing tree, use wine, nor construct any house… Some of them raise camels, others sheep, pasturing them in the desert…"

Diodorus of Sicily, *The Library of History*,
Book 19, 1st century BC,
translated by Russel M. Geer, 1954

CHAPTER 2
THE KINGDOM OF THE NABATAEANS

Left: an elaborate stele at Petra to "the goddess of Hayyan," as the inscription reads; right: a simple graffito from Wadi Rum. The symbolic repertoire of the Nabataeans is richer than was once thought.

The early record

The Greek historian Diodorus of Sicily describes the Nabataean people in the 4th century before the common era as living a rough and rural life, without cities or settled agriculture. His 1st-century BC report is based on the earlier "eyewitness" testimony of the historian Hieronymus of Cardia, who had served in the army of one of Alexander the Great's generals, Antigonus of Macedonia (382–301 BC), later a ruler in the Near East. Diodorus gives an account of two expeditions against the Nabataeans by Antigonus.

This impression seems to be contradicted by the Greek geographer Strabo, citing the philosopher Athenodorus, who visited Petra toward the beginning of the Christian era. He describes the metropolis of the Nabataeans as a great city with an abundance of water, gardens, and expensive stone houses.

These texts present the evidence of two contemporaneous Westerners who had direct contact with Petra. They allow us to imagine the discovery of the hidden city in ancient times by Europeans. Though in a different context, the experience of these first visitors is comparable to that of the European travelers at the beginning of the 19th century— they express the same surprise, the same desire to explore and explain, and a certain incomprehension, in particular regarding some alien social conventions. For example, Strabo tells us that Athenodorus was shocked by the proximity of the tombs to food-storage areas, and certain religious practices

Below: this group of musicians playing the lyre, the double aulos (similar to an oboe), and the tambourine are women. According to Strabo, female duets played at Nabataean banquets presided over by the king himself.

remained strange to him, though he attempted to understand them.

The origins of the Nabataeans

Like Strabo, Diodorus wrote for a Roman readership, and it was in relation to their Greco-Roman models that both writers saw the Nabataeans as exotic. The historical, linguistic, and archaeological research being conducted today strives to balance this enduring impression. Although there has never been a doubt that the Nabataeans were a part of the Arab world, their exact origins remain a question. Some scholars suggest that they were from the central or southern part of the Arabian peninsula; others that they came from Mesopotamia and the Persian Gulf region. More information about their early history is likely to be gleaned through exploration of central and northwestern Saudi Arabia, a land that remains for the most part little known to archaeologists. In this vast territory, indications may be found of when and how the Nabataeans first emerged from a group of nomadic Arabian tribes whose roots there are ancient. Relations between the Nabataeans and their near and distant neighbors, recorded in various families of extant Arabic inscriptions, must be clarified as well.

Left: a Renaissance-era "portrait" of Strabo. Little is known of the life of this writer, a Greek of Asiatic ancestry. He made numerous trips to Rome and traveled throughout the Mediterranean world. Few of his historical works survive, but his lengthy *Geography* is completely extant, and includes both information gathered by him and reports drawn from earlier books. In Book 16, in which he discusses Assyria, Babylon, Syria, and Arabia, we find detailed material on the Nabataeans. He describes their way of life in the course of recounting an unpleasant expedition to Arabia Felix, the land of incense, undertaken by Aelius Gallus, the Roman prefect in Egypt. Strabo conscientiously cites his sources, including Greeks such as the geographer Eratosthenes and the philosopher Athenodorus, who knew the region well, and who had stayed "in the home of the people of Petra and who spoke of it with admiration." Athenodorus was surprised to see the king serve guests with his own hands at official banquets, and concluded from this that Nabataean royalty had a "democratic" nature. He was aware of egalitarian tendencies in the Arab world, but apparently did not recognize a welcoming ritual that is still practiced there to this day.

We do know that by the end of the 4th century BC the growing caravan trade drew this people out from the closed universe of nomad herder society and into the world of international economic and political relations. To do so, the Nabataeans used Aramaic, the language of commerce throughout the Near East.

Masters of the caravan

Diodorus and Strabo agree on one point: the Nabataeans earned the bulk of their wealth from their commercial pursuits. The land on which they lived produced little more than copper from Wadi Araba and bitumen from the Dead Sea. The latter was transported to Egypt and sold for use in embalming the dead and caulking boats.

Unfortunately, the texts offer little information regarding the organization of Nabataean caravans. According to Strabo, they were immense, comprising so many men and camels that they resembled an army; they must have made a powerful impression. We do not know what other merchandise (besides copper and asphaltum) they carried on the outbound journey, but it is known they sought incense, myrrh, and certain spices from their

Above: myrrh was burned in rituals as an incense and used as a perfume. Nabataean caravans transported it the length of the desert routes. Below: the arid but beautiful terrain of Wadi Rum.

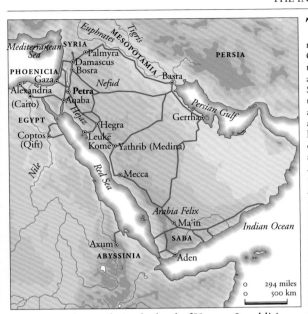

The Nabataeans commanded the caravan routes between Petra and Gaza, those leading across the Sinai to Alexandria, and those to southern Syria, but they controlled the routes in Arabia only as far south as Hegra, almost 300 miles (500 kilometers) from their capital. There, they forged a relationship with other Arabian tribes, who traveled the length of the Arabian peninsula—another 1,175 miles (2,000 kilometers)—to the kingdoms of the spice producers in Yemen, called Arabia the Fortunate by Diodorus and Arabia Felix by the Romans. From Hegra, too, these tribes crossed the peninsula to the Persian Gulf port of Gerrha, where spice ships embarked for India, and visited the Nabataean *emporium* at Leukē Komē on the Red Sea. Scholars praise the Nabataeans' talent as caravaners, but not their maritime skills. Strabo, however, spoke of them as sometimes engaging in piracy. Diodorus wrote: "The Nabataeans far surpass the others in wealth, although they are not much more than ten thousand in number; for not a few of them are accustomed to bring down to the sea frankincense and myrrh and the most valuable kinds of spices, which they procure from those who convey them from what is called Arabia the Fortunate."

partners to the south, in the land of Yemen. In addition, they bought the spices that arrived from India at Leukē Komē, which Strabo described as an important *emporium,* a market city or trading post.

These products traveled the route northward from the Hejaz and, passing through Hegra, arrived in Petra, which functioned as a transit point. From there they were conveyed to the Mediterranean ports, in particular Gaza and Alexandria. The most important route was that between Petra and Gaza; today it has been identified and defined clearly. The goods were then shipped to Greece and Italy, where they were highly valued for a range of uses, including religious rituals, medicines, beauty products, and cooking. The exorbitant prices these luxury commodities commanded explain the growing wealth of the Nabataeans and the progressive expansion of their domain along the principal caravan routes, where they sought to maintain control. This area included the Negev and Sinai to the south and, in the north, the far reaches of the Wadi Sirhan, a valley that marked the transport route to and from the Persian Gulf. This economic and territorial expansion attracted the interest of the Romans, themselves in a period of expansion, and was eventually one of the reasons that they imposed an alliance on Nabataea and later annexed it.

The Hellenistic period

The story of the Nabataeans unfolded in a Near East dominated by the confrontation of two Hellenistic monarchies, both born from the Alexandrian Empire: the Lagids in Egypt and the Seleucids in Syria. At the end of the 3d century BC, these two between them controlled the whole of the Syrian-Palestinian region. As long as they held power, the Nabataeans remained confined to the desert outreaches of Seleucia, the area immediately east of Petra. A single extant Nabataean inscription from this period, dating to 169–168 BC, mentions a local ruler: a King Aretas, perhaps Aretas I, the first known king of Nabataea.

Seleucid power gradually weakened, victim of internal dissension and pressure by the Romans; in this power vacuum new principalities developed under indigenous chiefs. As related by Diodorus and Strabo, the cultural revolution in Nabataean society between the 3d and 1st centuries BC was paralleled by an evolution of the political system, from a tribal organization in which the chief (the Greek term used is *phylarch*) had to negotiate his authority as first among equals, to a system more or less based upon the model of the Hellenistic monarchies. This shift is signaled in the source texts by a change in the word for "king" used to describe the ruler. The Greek title *tyrannos* is used for Aretas I; by the reign of Rabbel I (c. 87 BC) it is *basileus*. Nabataean kings also took royal epithets in the Hellenistic Greek style, such as Aretas III Philhellene, Rabbel II Life-Giver and Savior of His People.

A Hellenistic influence is also seen in the style of the coins minted by Nabataean kings. The first silver coins were issued by Aretas III (84–62 BC), a powerful ruler whose reign saw the greatest expansion of the Nabataean

Nabataean currency consisted solely of silver and bronze coins. Below: a silver coin depicting Aretas IV dates from the first year of his reign (9/8 BC). His name and official epithet, Lover of His People, run around the edge. Opposite below: a bronze coin depicts Rabbel II, the last Nabataean king, and his mother, Queen Shaqilat, who served as regent at the beginning of his reign, between AD 70 and 76. The frequent association of a king with a queen, whether a spouse or a mother, corresponds to a Hellenistic tradition especially in use in

Ptolemaic Alexandria. It underscored the continuity and independence of the dynasty.

inscription_fragment

Left: this fragment of inscription found in Petra commemorates a "construction made by… son of Diodorus, chief of the cavalry…in honor of Aretas, [king of Nab] ataea, and Queen Haganu, [the daughter of] Malichus, king of Nabataea" in AD 10. The Nabataean cavalry was famous; chief of cavalry was an important position held by an officer close to the sovereign. The inscription dates from the reign of the great king Aretas IV, who acceded to the throne in 9 BC. He did so only after great difficulties, due to the intrigues of the minister Syllaeus and the opposition of Rome, whose influence at the time was decisive.

kingdom into the north. In 84 BC, the merchants of Damascus invited him to rule over their city, to protect their caravans from predation by other Arab tribes, such as the Itureans, from the neighboring Bekaa Valley of Lebanon and upper Jordan. The Nabataean king thus seems to have been seen as a trusty and efficient regional custodian.

Rome against the Nabataeans

By the 1st century BC, the Jewish kingdom of the Hasmonaeans in Palestine had become the Nabataeans' principal territorial adversary, meddling in their rivals' internal conflicts and supporting various opposition clans in

Jerusalem. These interventions led to confrontations with Rome, which, under the military leadership of Pompey (106–48 BC), had definitively established itself as a power in the Near East after 63 BC. Petra was besieged and Nabataea suffered many invasions during the reigns of kings Obodas II (c. 62–60) and Malichus I (60–30). Retaliating in 25–24 BC, Obodas III thwarted a Roman invasion into southern Arabia.

In reaction, the Romans, having discovered that seasonal monsoon winds allowed them to sail up the Red Sea, developed an alternative route for their incense,

This tomb carved into the cliff of al-Khubtha at Petra is that of the Roman governor Titus Aninius Sextius Florentinus, "imperial legate pro-praetor of the Province of Arabia." It is located near a series of great sepulchers of princes.

detouring commercial traffic to ports on the Egyptian shore of the Red Sea and from there by caravan to the Nile and thence to Alexandria, the principal Mediterranean terminus for commodities going to Europe. Their aim was to bypass intermediaries and thus boost their profits. In so doing, they undermined the desert caravan trade, whose final stops were Nabataean. It was perhaps during this phase that the Nabataeans began to focus new efforts on agricultural exploitation of the most fertile lands under their authority, such as the area around Bosra, in southern Syria. The reign of Aretas IV (9 BC–AD 40) marked the apogee of the kingdom's prosperity; this seems to have been the period in which vast construction projects, notably at Petra, were undertaken. Under his successors Malichus II (AD 40–70) and Rabbel II (AD 70–106), who made Bosra (which they called Bostra) a second capital, Roman influence grew.

An inscription in Latin high over the entryway of his tomb provides some information regarding the career of Sextius Florentinus, who is otherwise little known. He had been the legate of the Legion of Brittany, quaestor in Achaea, and proconsul of South Gaul. It is thought that he was governor of Arabia during the reign of Emperor Hadrian, between AD 126 and 130, and that he died in Petra without achieving the rank of consul. Although the administrative seat of the new Roman province had by then been moved to Bosra, it is known that, at least early on, governors continued to convene regular meetings at the old capital, which held the rank of metropolis. A set of papyri discovered near the Dead Sea (legal documents called the Archives of Babbatha, relating to a woman of the region) make reference to this. In time, Petra was used less and less by the Roman governors.

The "end" of Nabataea

As Rome grew dominant, it at first kept the Nabataean dynasty in place as a client kingdom, but in 106 the emperor Trajan established direct administration by creating the province of Arabia, with an administrative seat in Bosra (in what is now southern Syria), rather than Petra. Petra nevertheless survived. But though it was situated near a new route that Trajan forged to relink Bosra with Aqaba on the Red Sea, it was no longer a major caravan center—traffic having been rerouted through Palmyra—and became a mere secondary city of the Eastern Roman Empire. Great urban projects there nevertheless attest to its prosperity during the long period of relative tranquillity that followed, called the Pax Romana, or Roman Peace. At the end of the 4th century, an administrative reorganization of the Eastern Empire transformed Petra into the capital—given the official title of "metropolis"—of a new province named Palaestina Tertia. When Christianity took hold in the area, it became the see of the local bishopric. Churches of this period at Petra, richly decorated with mosaics in the Byzantine manner, show that the city remained a lively center in the Byzantine period, despite several earthquakes in the 4th and 5th centuries. (Earthquakes have been documented in 363 and 419, and it was long thought that these had caused Petra to be abandoned.) Over these centuries, however, the nucleus of the indigenous Nabataean population, identifiable through family names recorded in papyri, seems to have merged with the Arabians who continually came to settle in the area.

The entire region became Islamic in the 630s, but information about this period is scant. The city did not enjoy the cultural flowering that took place elsewhere in the Mideast at this time; devastating

For a long time, no Christian churches were known at Petra, despite the fact that the city had continued to thrive in the early Christian period. But in 1990, a joint American-Jordanian expedition excavated the foundations of a 5th-century church in the center of the city.

earthquakes, in particular one in 747, progressively emptied it of inhabitants. The few medieval sources at our disposal, Frankish and Arabic chronicles, scarcely mention the city's population and refer only to forts constructed there in the 12th century.

The Nabataean territory

It is difficult to demarcate the precise limits of Nabataea from ancient sources because its borders were continually changing. Nevertheless, we can identify a continuous nucleus that corresponds to the ancient kingdom of Edom in southern Jordan, and can further define zones abutting this, over which the Nabataeans exercised authority. The reign of Aretas III over Damascus between 84 and 72 BC represents Nabataea's widest expansion. And we can assume that at the peripheries the monarchy exercised less territorial sovereignty than supervision over caravan routes, in particular the Arabian route, whose southernmost Nabataean stops were Hegra (Medain Saleh), in the Hejaz, and Leukē Komē on the Red Sea, about halfway down the Arabian Peninsula. Other Arabian tribes secured the route farther to the south.

The Nabataeans also transported goods across inland roads in the Negev desert, from the Persian Gulf to Gaza, and from Ma'in in Arabia Felix, far to the south. The evidence of a Nabataean presence along this route is clear (one of the most ancient Nabataean inscriptions has been found there); and we may surmise that they probably controlled it politically, at least to some extent. This region also enjoyed as much agricultural development as the land around Petra, but it has not been proven that this dates from the Nabataean period. Ancient authors also mention the presence of Nabataeans in the country

Opposite: the church incorporated both Nabataean and Roman architectural elements. The plan is that of a basilica with three naves, each ending in a semi-circular apse, preceded by a porticoed atrium. The aisles are paved with mosaics with motifs of medallions, containing images of baskets, vases, and animals surrounded by symbolic figures such as personifications of Ocean and the seasons. Adjacent to the church is a complex of rooms. In one of these an important set of papyri dating from the 5th and 6th centuries was discovered. Though charred in a fire at the end of the 6th century, they have proved essential in understanding the Byzantine period in the region. Above: the personification of Summer, a detail of the pavement.

of Midian, east of the Gulf of Aqaba, and at Leukē Komē. Important Nabataean ruins and artifacts have been discovered at Qasrawet in the Sinai, on the caravan road to Alexandria.

We also know that Nabataea controlled a part of southern Syria. Ancient Bosra, the second capital of the kingdom, has been identified with an archaeological site there by numerous finds of painted Nabataean ceramicware, which is very rare elsewhere in the Hauran. But the most telling signs that this was a Nabataean city are some impressive and characteristically Nabataean works of architecture—especially a monumental arch and a large edifice, possibly a sanctuary, with graceful Corinthian capitals—that seem to follow a true Nabataean city plan.

In the region extending from Bosra to Hegra, inscriptions have been found referring to "Dushara, god of our Master, who is in Bosra." This "Master" was Rabbel II, the last king prior to the Roman annexation. He increased the role of the region in Nabataean affairs, and these dedications indicate that

At its most extensive, the Nabataean kingdom comprised central and southern Jordan (the ancient lands of Moab and Edom), the Negev as far as the ports of Gaza and Rhinocolura, southern Syria, and spurs of territory along the trade routes in the Sinai that led to Alexandria and Arabia.

Left: the Nabataean Gate stands at the center of Bosra. Like all architecture in the region, it is built of basalt blocks. Its date is late 1st century AD, and it is a classicizing interpretation of Nabataean style, with its horned capital. This monumental public work is a hallmark of the remodeling of the city carried out by the last Nabataean kings. Bosra is situated on fertile land; it became the second capital of Nabataea under Rabbel II, whose epithet, Life-Giver and Savior of His People, may signify that he brought a new prosperity to the Nabataeans, who suffered a decline when the Romans diverted a portion of their caravan traffic to Alexandria through a sea route.

a dynastic Nabataean cult was established in Bosra, where Dushara was identified with the local deity Aarra.

As we examine this evidence, a far-reaching and diverse Nabataean world emerges, cohesive despite ill-defined and shifting borders. One mark of the existence of a unified culture is the discovery throughout much of this area of numerous cult references citing the "god of Shera," the principal cult of Petra.

Arabian divinities and syncretism

The Nabataeans had a polytheistic religion of indigenous Arabian origin, whose pantheon was dominated by Dushara, the god of Shera, the mountain that towers to the east of Petra and Gaia (today the village of Wadi Musa). He was the protector of the royal dynasty. A 10th-century Byzantine lexicon called the *Sonda* describes his baetyl (cult object) and the blood sacrifices that took place in his temple.

From the same pre-Islamic Arabian source (although his precise origins remain in dispute) arose al-Kutbâ, the god of writing and divination. A triad of goddesses, Allat (the name means "the goddess"), al-'Uzza ("the Very Strong"), and Manawât, surround Allah (or al-Ilah, "the

The sandstone heights of Hegra are peppered with eighty-one large tombs with very tall facades and with rock-hewn sanctuaries similar to those at Petra. Above: the Tomb of el-Khusruf. Located near an oasis, the town was the final major stop on the route to Arabia Felix. The topography of Hegra is the opposite of Petra's: the site is an enormous rock massif that shoots up from a vast expanse of open sand. Each set of tombs bears a name.

god"). But the Nabataeans also adopted several divinities from earlier peoples who had been in the region, including the Edomite god and the Syrian god Ba'alshamin. A dedication to Atargatis, goddess of Menbidj, in northern Syria, can still be read in an inscription at Petra. As the cult of the Greco-Roman pantheon spread through the Mideast (mainly in the wake of Alexander the Great), it entered local cultures in a variety of ways. Assimilation was not always immediate, and was anything but mechanical; often it became quite complicated. For example, Dushara is sometimes identified with Dionysus, sometimes with Zeus; but Zeus is also sometimes seen as the equivalent of Ba'alshamin. Al-Kutbâ is associated with Hermes/Mercury, Allat with Athene/Minerva, Manawât with Fate or Nemesis, and al-'Uzza, who was worshiped especially in the Sinai and Negev, with Aphrodite Urania/Venus Caelestis (though Allat is sometimes also equated with

The walls of the Siq bear the signs of centuries of passing visitors. In the Roman era, festival leaders called panegyrarchs came from Adraa (modern Deraa) in southern Syria to take part in the festivals of Dushara at the capital, and carved their names there in Greek. Above: a baetyl of Dushara of Adraa is cut into the rock face. Its characteristic ovoid form is also found on the coins of that city. An anthropomorphic representation of a Syrian god or goddess that had also been sculpted in a niche was destroyed by iconoclasts.

these). Al-'Uzza is even sometimes linked with the Egyptian goddess Isis, who held great standing in Petra, where Alexandrian influence is evident.

Many other cults endured until they were overwhelmed by the Christian expansion during the 4th and 5th centuries AD, and some even survived in the Hejaz and elsewhere until the advent of Islam.

Iconography played a determining role in many of these links between the traditional religion and that of Hellenistic Greece. The principal divine image of the former was the baetyl, a cult object characteristic of pre-Islamic Arabian belief systems, primarily from the Middle East. These standing stones were not the representation of a divinity but, more precisely, the sign of the presence of the divine. Such objects occasionally appear in the monotheistic religions: the stone of Jacob in the Old Testament and the Kaaba of Mecca in Islam are derived from the same tradition. As the Nabataeans became a settled culture, receptive to the Greco-Roman world, imported divine images and those inspired by classical models proliferated alongside the baetyls, without completely supplanting them.

Nabataean traditions, with their deep Arabian roots inherited from the nomadic past, persisted in later periods. They remained vital despite the radical change that the settling process represented. A determining element in this transformation was the choice and domestication of a rather unlikely site for a city: that of Petra.

L eft: this bust of a bearded god wearing a broad crown, set within a medallion, is Dushara. It is a good example of the anthropomorphic representational style (that is, the representation of gods in human form), which has nothing in common with the baetyl images, although the two were contemporaneous. The animated expression on this figure's face is not typical of the Hellenistic Greek style.

B elow: at Khirbet Tannur a goddess crowned with fish or dolphins (in other images she wears ears of corn) adorns the pilaster of a temple. Her name may be Derketo, who became conflated with the Syrian goddess

Atargatis, whose cult reached as far as Nabataea.

Today, archaeologists are examining Petra and its environs for details of the lives of its people. Gradually, they are building an understanding of the living city. One is struck by the vastness and intelligence of the urban systems that the Nabataeans achieved, in order to create a city in such an inhospitable site, and then to maintain and defend it. To master an environment so difficult required a great talent for adaptation on the part of these former nomads.

CHAPTER 3
FROM REFUGE TO CARAVAN CAPITAL

Left: the great urn crowning ad-Deir overlooks the variegated sandstone massifs that border the Petra basin. Right: the face of a man or god found in Khirbet Tannur is by an artist working in the indigenous Eastern tradition, as indicated by the stylized, geometric treatment and the importance of the gaze.

An archaeologist's perspective

Enchanted by the strangeness of the site, with its monuments carved dramatically into the living rock, the first explorers of Petra were captivated by the rock-hewn tombs and great religious buildings. There was not much else to be seen at the time, so these early scholars surmised that Petra had never been a city, but was merely a necropolis and a large sanctuary.

In the first phase of archaeology, the daily life of the town excited little interest. Few attempts were made to study the means by which the Nabataean people, in a particularly difficult environment, fed themselves, moved about, secured their defense, and developed a social, political, and religious identity. Yet one can only understand the living Petra when one ceases to think of this site as different in all ways from other cities and pursues normal archaeological and historical investigation. To learn more about the city's quotidian life in no way diminishes its fascination.

Some archaeologists study the terrain beyond the city. The texts of Diodorus and Strabo suggest a new avenue of research here: the utilization of space by the Nabataeans at each stage of their history. How did they master the harsh desert environment and its meager resources to create cultivated cropland and an urban nucleus, while at the same time transforming their way of life? Upon what technical experience could they draw to manage water and land and construct a city? What was the effect of these changes upon their culture, and what do the surviving inscriptions and works of art reveal about them? In the absence of more explicit texts, this space has retained the strongest traces of the technological revolution that occurred between the end of the 4th century BC and the advent of the Christian era.

After 150 years, excavations have still barely penetrated the surface of the site. Before these could be expanded, it was necessary to create an exhaustive mapped inventory of all its elements. This task was undertaken at the beginning of the century, but at that time the primary interest was in the monuments. New documents that cover many categories of research are now available.

Beyond ad-Deir lie massifs of sandstone, granite, and porphyry sliced by steep ravines.

Overleaf: an illustration of the route taken by visitors through Petra. Beginning at far lower right and moving left along the Siq gorge, we see the Djinn Tombs; to their left are the Obelisk Tomb and the Bab el-Siq Triclinium. Proceeding along the aisle of the Siq, El Khazneh is at bottom center. Above this are the theater and the Tomb of Uneishu. Past the theater the Wadi Musa stream bends right (north) and then left (west), where it runs through the Colonnaded Street (the principal east–west avenue) to the lower city. To the north is the road to the Turkmaniyya Tomb and Jabal ad-Deir, crowned with the Monastery Tomb (upper left). Above and to the right of the Colonnaded Street rise the great facades of the Urn Tomb and other tombs cut into the tall cliffs of al-Khubtha, one of the city's formal High Places, or acropolises. Past the lower city is the path that ascends to the peak of Jabal Umm al-Biyara. One descends back to the basin floor along the Wadi Farasa, passing, at bottom left, the Garden Tomb, the Tomb of the Roman Soldier, and the Renaissance Tomb.

Extensive aerial photographic surveys and satellite images have been completed, leading to the identification of new areas of exploration; these have yielded more than 3,200 archaeological elements, ranging from a dam on a stream, to a quarry, to a simple inscription. Close study of their distribution enables us to understand the Nabataean exploitation of land and organization of Petra and its environs.

A paradoxical site

One point is key: the model upon which urban space is organized differs from that of the traditional cities of the Mediterranean and Near East. In Petra, artifacts are dispersed over an area some 7 miles (12 kilometers) in diameter, with concentrations in the center and some hubs along the periphery. The precise limits of the city are difficult to define. In most classical cities, the interior areas were the political, judicial, and religious precincts and are clearly distinguishable from exterior areas. Ramparts generally separated the two zones. For good

Below: the theater was enlarged several times and then returned to its original state, perhaps during the reign of Aretas IV. To dig tiers that could hold 3,000 to 6,000 spectators, the builders cut through a former necropolis in an area south of the theater known as the Streets of Facades, where 44 tombs of differing types run the lengths of four superimposed terraces. This sector shows well the range of projects carried out in Nabataean times that entailed cutting into the cliffs, and took advantage of the multilevel terrain, with its faults and salients.

Left: viewed from the summit of Jabal Madhbah in the southeast, the lower city spreads out on either side of the Colonnaded Street, within its circle of mountains. On the far side stands Jabal ad-Deir and, lower down, the acropolis of al-Habis, which also has a medieval fort, built by European Crusaders. Though it is one of the city's formal High Places, it appears to squat at the foot of the immense table mountain Umm al-Biyara, the "mother of cisterns," that dominates the countryside, rising to a height of 985 feet (300 meters). This massif is very difficult of access, and has been tentatively identified with a site, sometimes called Sela, mentioned in the Bible (Numbers 24:21, II Kings 14:7, Isaiah 16:1); it was probably also the original Rock from which early Petra took its name. Excavations have brought to light the remains of a 7th-century BC Edomite settlement, large cisterns, and a Nabataean religious place. It is here that the early nomadic Nabataeans stored their wealth and took refuge in times of danger.

defense, a classical city was situated in an elevated position, if possible with its inner city on a high central hill, or acropolis. Petra, however, lies at the bottom of a natural basin, or cirque, approximately 1¾ x 3 miles (3 x 5 kilometers) in area, dominated on all sides by vast heights.

Further, a classical city lies near a spring or river, ensuring a regular water supply and arable land that can furnish at least part of its subsistence. There is such a site about 3½ miles (6 kilometers) east of Petra, near a group of springs that includes the Ain Musa ("Spring of Moses"). These irrigated a zone of gardens and cultivated

terraces, which were also well watered by rain runoff from the slopes of Jabal Shera. Today, the village of Wadi Musa stands here. Part of this site is on raised land and could have been fortified in the classical manner. Furthermore, it is near the traditional route that leads north from the Gulf of Aqaba, the renowned and age-old "route of the kings." Normally, a classical city was situated upon such a road. Petra is detached from all the routes in the region, and passage to many of them is difficult. We must try to understand why this peculiar and awkward site was chosen for the construction of an important transit city, rather than Wadi Musa, which had so many obvious assets.

From refuge to city

The account of Diodorus sheds some light on the question. He notes that the place was called in Greek *hē Petra* (the name means "the rock"), and that in 312 BC a Greek general, Athenaeus, attempted to seize it. In its origins, it was not a city in the classical sense, but the refuge of a nomadic tribe, herders and caravaners who dwelt in an area of rough terrain and urgently needed a secure place to store their accumulated riches. It provided a fixed reference point for a people constantly on the move, and as such it became the

home of religious institutions and funerary monuments.

That Petra's founders were nomads explains some of the characteristic traits that the city retains. The major task of the Nabataeans was to transform this primitive natural refuge into a city, with a different level of status. They had to find the resources to feed it and the means to defend it. They needed to develop new kinds of dwellings for the population as well as for their gods, to organize traffic, and to demarcate zones for the living and for the dead. In these matters their Hellenized neighbors and, later, the Romanized cities of the Near East provided examples. However, in many instances the Nabataeans found their own solutions.

The mastery of water

To create a city, one begins by assuring the availability of fundamental resources, especially

The entry to Petra is a narrow fissure no more than 40 feet (12 meters) wide, with walls reaching an elevation of as much as 330 feet (100 meters). Its length, its sinuous path, and the sheer height of its walls combine to make an access route that was particularly easy to defend, reinforcing the impression of the site as a natural fortress. Some areas have been uncovered that were paved with cobblestones. Its walls are lined with incised niches and dedications. The mysterious atmosphere, sometimes oppressively shadowed, accentuates the sense that this is truly a "sacred way." Above: the mouth of the Siq, seen from the porch of El Khazneh.

water. Petra has springs that flow continually, but these provide only a nominal output. The collection of rainwater had to augment this supply. But in this semiarid desert climate, rain is very infrequent. It was therefore necessary to gather it on the broadest surface possible. This may explain why the city lies at the bottom of a broad, sloping bowl, surrounded by steep cliffs.

When rain falls upon a basin 54 square miles (92 square kilometers) in area, on hard terrain that absorbs very

From the time of the Nabataeans, lateral fissures and narrow ravines on either side of the Siq were transformed into access roads leading to the upper venues. Left: staircases and precipitous, narrow tracks were cut into the sandstone. These could easily be obstructed and defended. Due to severe erosion, some can now only barely be discerned. Similar structures can be found in all the ravines and upon all the heights of Petra and its environs, particularly around the principal High Places and ad-Deir. As with all cities that incorporate hills, many of the "streets" of Petra are flights of stairs, though steeper and more dramatic than in most towns. In such uneven terrain, between rugged cliffs and flat plains, traffic patterns could not be organized according to a classical scheme of central square (agora or forum) and parallel or converging streets. The street plan of Petra undoubtedly evolved from several nuclei.

little, water will amass
in a few hours in considerable
and sometimes dangerous
amounts. Rainfall into the
basin of Petra flows along the
course of the unchanneled Wadi Musa, which also
continually carried water into the city from the Ain Musa,
the most abundant spring in the area.

A systematic exploration of the entire zone of Petra has
revealed a great variety of sophisticated structures for the
collection, control, and distribution of water. Conceived
with intelligence, these were based on close analysis of
the topography, which is highly irregular. Water collected
from the surfaces of the rocks was carried by rock-cut
channels, or occasionally conduits constructed of stone,
or covered with stone slabs, into open-air reservoirs or
closed cisterns.

Some of these waterworks were modest in size and
could be maintained by a small number of people at the
domestic level. Larger systems included dams, organized
in chains, that blocked the gorges leading into the basin
and supplied the reservoirs. These installations were
complemented by a network of long-distance conduits
that carried water to Petra from the most important
springs in the area, which rose several kilometers away
at the edge of the plateau, to districts well above the
water level of the Wadi Musa. This system reveals an
impressive technical mastery. A project of such large
scope was surely beyond the capabilities of a small
community.

An extensive network
of water pipes was
implemented in the
northeastern and
southeastern sectors of
the city to collect,
channel, and distribute
the water from springs
located several miles
away. Top: these water
ducts are depicted in a
sketch by René Saupin.
Extant elements of the
conduits indicate that
they were built on a
smooth, carefully
calculated slope that
reveals a remarkable
command of hydraulic
technology. Above: a
piece of terra-cotta pipe;
conduits were either
pipes or gutters carved
into the rock and
rendered watertight by a
hydraulic plaster made of
lime, sometimes mixed
with clay.

Another impressive public project was the protection of the narrow passage of the Siq from the violent flooding to which it was exposed. This was accomplished by diverting the overflow of the Wadi Musa through a tunnel into a tributary. The Nabataeans clearly mastered water conservation and management at Petra in progressive stages.

Agricultural development

This water, stored in cisterns, was used primarily for consumption by the inhabitants and their cattle, but also to irrigate gardens. Traces of agricultural development remain quite visible around Petra. There are some classical-style cultivation terraces in the district near the modern village of Wadi Musa. A more unusual system of staged dams cut off the flow of watercourses in the small wadis, forcing rainwater to seep into the

Top: after the Wadi Musa stream was diverted, a channel carved into the left side of the Siq carried water from the abundant spring of Ain Braq to the city. Above: the Nabataeans also became masters in the art of making and maintaining cisterns.

surrounding alluvial ground. This program of soil conservation remained effective as long as the dams were regularly maintained. Most of them burst or were swept away following the abandonment of the site. A third kind of system is found in a district oddly called the "Roman gardens," though its irrigation method is closer to those used in southern Arabia. Here, a bypass canal and low dividing walls were built to manage water distribution.

There is little information regarding what foodstuffs the people of Petra cultivated, though these probably included cereals. Traces of barley and wheat have been found in the surrounding area, some dating as far back as the Neolithic period. In addition, there were probably fruit trees and perhaps grapes, since presses have been found cut into the rock. They certainly bred sheep and goats, and perhaps camels and horses were to be seen in the pasturelands of Wadi Musa and Beidha. In other regions of Nabataea, near the Dead Sea and in the oases of the Sinai and Arabia, palm trees proliferated. Grapes grew well in the Negev, and the fertile region of southern Syria was known for its wheat, as well as other crops.

All of these waterworks and agricultural systems are still far from being dated with any certainty. In any case, they were indispensable to the growth of an important urban center. That Petra thrived between the 1st century BC and the 2d century AD is suggested both by the number of great monuments dating from that time and by recently uncovered evidence regarding the development of living conditions.

It is surprising to see a people whose traditions were nomadic succeed at and perfect such an ambitious project, not only by exploiting available resources

Below: in a banquet hall in the Siq al-Barid, or "small Siq," located several miles north of Petra, the vaulted ceiling is painted in fresco with motifs of birds, small cupids, and a young flute player surrounded by laden grapevines. This decoration suggests the importance of grapes and wine to the Nabataeans, as emphasized in Strabo, who speaks of wine being drunk from golden goblets. Numerous archaeological discoveries support the presumption of a significant viniculture at Petra.

Zurrabeh, in the environs of Petra, was laid out in cultivated terraces, many of which date to the Nabataean period. These are most clearly visible around the present-day village of Wadi Musa and along the road between Petra and Shaubak. Following the contours of the land in easy levels, they are covered with small fields, gardens, and orchards. This classical system, in widespread use in the ancient world, makes the most of irregular terrain. The Nabataeans, however, used terracing in conjunction with other methods less familiar elsewhere in the Mediterranean: limiting erosion and conserving and amassing fertile soil through control of the watercourses' alluvial deposits. The range and ingenuity of these systems reveal the remarkable ability of the Nabataeans to adapt to the land, in an effort to ensure the survival and prosperity of an important urban center.

skillfully—which itself entailed a minute observation of the terrain—but also by fully mastering the complex technology of hydraulics. For some of their projects, the Nabataeans could call upon their own earlier experiences. Diodorus emphasized their talent for digging watertight and carefully concealed cisterns, as well as their general aptitude for management of water in the desert. These skills dated to their nomadic past.

Two of the three methods for soil improvement found at Petra are clearly distinguished from the conventions of the Mediterranean world. Upon what technical tradition

B elow: today Petra is dotted with herds of small black goats, whose domestication in the area may date to the Neolithic era. In Beidha, signs indicate that cultivation of barley and wheat also

were they based—those of the settled Edomite farmers occupying the region prior to the arrival of the Nabataeans, or those of the much more distant populations of southern Syria, where these methods of irrigation have also been documented? It is worth noting that one of the most celebrated agronomic treaties of the medieval Arabian world refers to the Nabataeans.

An original defense system

The same sense of observation and efficient utilization of the terrain can be seen in the perfection of an original defense system adapted to this complex site. Diodorus, writing of an earlier period, describes a much less developed defense system than does Strabo. Both writers stress the fact that Petra was not defended

dates to this period. Above: this millstone attests to the continuation of grain production through the Roman period.

by classical ramparts, but rather was fortified by nature itself. (Although some lines of ramparts do exist, apparently delimiting the lower city at its northern and southern reaches, these most probably date from the late Roman period.)

Indeed, a continuous defensive wall would have had to cover a great length and been manned by guards spaced too far apart to be effective. The Nabataeans instead chose a mobile and fluid defensive strategy that relied upon fortified points which served principally as observation and communication posts. Some towers have been identified around the periphery of Petra, in particular on the peak looking toward Arabia, whence, Diodorus says, the principal threat came. He also described the Nabataeans' tactics quite precisely. When Antigonus's Greeks were planning to attack the city for the second time, their captain, Demetrius, "advanced for three days through regions with no roads, striving not to be observed by the barbarians; but the lookouts, having seen that a hostile force had entered, informed the Nabataeans by means of prearranged fire signals." This tactic, adapted for the desert, must have its roots in their nomadic history. The defense of Petra remained dependent mainly on a system of small forts placed at strategic points within the city limits, along its periphery, at the outlets of the valleys leading toward Arabia, and on the summits of the inaccessibly steep slopes above it. Thus it is significant that Petra lies at the western edge of the Arabian plateau, whose high massifs and ridges form a natural barrier that protected it from invasions coming from the west. This too was undoubtedly a factor in the original choice of the site.

At the cost of carrying out substantial development

Left: the plunging gorges of the Wadi Sleisel to the northwest of Petra are impressive. The peak housed either a small fort or an observation post. Indeed, this was the command point that oversaw the system of signal communications and messengers. Passages have been found in the rock too steep to have been used for other purposes.

projects, the Nabataeans of Petra methodically ensured the control of their territory and its resources. The discrepancy between the accounts of Diodorus and Strabo reveals the degree of change that occurred in an interval of three centuries of progressive settlement and urbanization. In that time, the way of life of at least a part of the population changed substantially, and along with it the cultural and political values of the Nabataeans. An analysis of the great hydraulic, strategic, and architectural projects accomplished at Petra, and the Hellenistic imagery of power inscribed in them, suggests that the culture developed a strong and organized authority.

Below: high cliffs stand to the east and south of Petra. From its earliest role as a place of temporary refuge, the city retained a unique topographic characteristic: the incorporation and use of high points of land within the city center, despite dramatic differences of altitude and terrain. Recent studies of the distribution of buildings make this feature all the more apparent.

In this unique urban space, a congeries of constructed and rock-hewn religious buildings, tombs, and homes, the vital Orientalism of the architecture is enriched with Greco-Roman influences. A compound style is apparent, too, in artworks and the crafts of the artisans. Skilled at borrowing and imitating, the Nabataeans succeeded in creating their own style.

CHAPTER 4
ANATOMY OF A CITY

Left: an aerial view of the southern necropolises shows the deep sculpting of the mountains carried out by the ancient tomb architects. Right: a fragment of a frieze with a motif of a soldier is distinctly Hellenistic in style, from the tilted pose of the head to the long, rippling locks of hair.

The fabric of the city

In Petra, the urban space was discontinuous. The population was dispersed in nuclei that more or less moved from the center toward the periphery. This rather haphazard plan is explained by the environmental constraints of the site: the city needed to make the most of limited and fragmented areas of arable land and restricted water resources; the instruments used for water collection, such as dams and cisterns, had to be sited with accuracy, according to the topography. The plan also conveys the history of the site's occupation by a

Top: the tombs of al-Khubtha and a sector of the lower city.

population in transition. A map of the residential area, together with one of the religious and burial places, yields insight into Petra's social organization and other aspects of Nabataean culture.

The center of the ancient city, called the lower city, was located on either side of the Wadi Musa, which runs through the center of the Petra basin. The main-axis street, densely built up, closely follows the watercourse. This area is far from being flat and regular, however. Great religious and public monuments mount in terraces

on the two facing slopes; beneath these are clusters of houses that scale the heights, split by ravines. These residential zones continue along the length of the wadis and access roads as far as the necropolises that (as is typical of Greco-Roman cities) lie at the edge of town, and sometimes beyond.

From tent to house: the ez-Zantur district

It is the private house that most clearly reveals the change in Nabataean culture from the nomadic to the urban. Athenodorus, quoted by Strabo, was struck by the opulence of the stone houses of Petra. At times, archaeologists doubted the existence of such grand homes, since they were buried under debris, impossible to identify before excavations were carried out. Whereas the poorer houses, troglodytic (cave, or rock-hewn) structures, were always visible, and thus were the first to be inventoried. A third house form, the tent dwelling, had been posited but until very recently was undocumented. However, Swiss excavations in the ez-Zantur district, on the dominant slope south of the monument center, have now uncovered

Opposite below: a large Nabataean house, excavated on the hill of ez-Zantur, was built during the 1st century AD on the site of a smaller two-room house of the previous century. A flat roof made of layers of clay, matting, and wood covered the left, or public section, with its banquet hall. An open-air atrium (1) and a vestibule, or small colonnaded courtyard (2), let light and air into the house. The floor in this area was partly covered with regular octagonal paving stones of limestone, the walls were stuccoed and painted (left: a detail), and the columns were crowned with the local version of a Corinthian capital. The private section of the house was much less refined, and was accessible only through a narrow doorway. The bedrooms were dark and small, reflecting the lifestyle of a Mideastern family. The courtyard to the right (3) was used for utilitarian purposes. Destroyed in a fire at the beginning of the 2d century and reconstructed around 300, the house was again destroyed in the earthquakes of 363 and 419.

successive states of a group of houses and have even established chronological reference points that mark the transition from a nomadic to a settled lifestyle.

Indeed, they have identified three major phases in the housing in this district. The oldest level corresponds to the seasonal encampments for which Petra was used until the end of the 2d century BC. This consists of layers of deposits of artifacts and graves. The second level is a stone construction, in turn superseded by an immense, well-paved stone house that dates to the 1st century BC. A large part of this building was used for public and social events; these rooms were laid out in the Hellenistic Mediterranean style, with peristyle and columned vestibule, and decorated with wall paintings. The private quarters, on the other hand, were arranged in an irregular fashion around a courtyard, in the Eastern manner.

This site indicates the way the residential areas of Petra began to take shape. Although some modest stone houses certainly existed in the lower city along the Colonnaded Street by the 3d century BC, seasonal occupancy in tents continued in other districts through the end of the 2d. The development of more luxurious homes, influenced by Hellenistic models, seems to have gone hand in hand with the great projects of monumental architecture.

Only small fragments of Petra's painted stucco survive, but it was evidently quite widespread throughout the city and indeed in all the sandstone sites of Nabataea. It was used in private residences as well as larger public buildings and served as a good protection for the brittle rock. The motifs, with their colored panels, delicately sculpted moldings, and occasional use of perspective effects, are often reminiscent of those found in the Hellenistic Mediterranean. Left: a painted wall from a rock-hewn residence at Wadi Siyyagh.

Rock-hewn dwellings

The cliffs of the basin are pocked with rock-hewn dwellings, comprising five or six hundred rooms. These early homes constituted a stage in the settling process of the nomads. Even today, Beduins occasionally use the stone-cut grottos, rooms, and tombs around Petra to store their belongings and provisions, though most of them live in tents or in a nearby modern town. The cliffs are composed of hard and soft strata of sandstone; the cave dwellings were sited to make use of this. Caves were dug in the softer layers of stone, where the cutting was easier; the hard layers became sturdy ceilings. Thus, the geology of the cliffs also played a part in the arrangement of the city, which grew as a complex network of cave houses and built houses. And it is likely that tent dwellings also existed.

The heterogeneous nature of housing in Petra and the interrupted, uneven use of urban space make any attempt at estimating the size of the population particularly

Above: the complex known as the House of Dorotheos (the name appears on it in a Greek inscription), comprises some twenty rooms dug into a northwest face of the Khubtha mountain, accessible by a staircase and lit by windows. The complex may have been the home of a wealthy citizen. There are a large triclinium and a terrace decorated with niches, baetyls, and altars dedicated to household gods. According to Strabo, the Nabataeans practiced sun worship on the roofs of their houses.

difficult. It is thought that something like 10,000 to 20,000 inhabitants lived there at the city's zenith. Diodorus said that there were "scarcely more than 10,000 people," but was writing of a period when the Nabataeans were still nomads.

An Eastern urban model

A Greek or Roman city divides a well-defined and uninterrupted space into orderly plots, with separate zones reserved for public and private use. Cities such as Petra and Palmyra—the other great caravan city of the Near East—evolved differently. In the beginning, groups (whether families or tribes) settled in a scattered fashion about the site, each building a house at a distance from its neighbors, so as to have room to expand. Thus, the urban fabric became progressively more dense at the expense of public space, bits of which survived in the form of small, irregular lanes, sometimes narrowing, sometimes broadening, and sometimes coming to a dead end. This form of urban development is ancient in the East, and has been identified in city centers dating as far back as the Bronze Age, if not earlier. It persisted in the traditional Eastern city, to the fascination of 19th-century European travelers.

A greco-Roman city underwent an evolution from a small agglomeration of groups scattered across a site to a politically unified urban entity, called in Greek a *polis*, or in Latin a *civitas*. It was often the sanctuaries that served as the unifying element. Around the beginning of the common era, there was a shift in the urban development of many cities: a principal sanctuary was built whose spectacular change in scale set it apart from all others. In Petra, this was the 1st-century BC Qasr al-Bint, an immense temple at the head of the Colonnaded Street, beneath the Umm al-

Above: the imposing structure of the Qasr al-Bint rises some 75 feet (23 meters) over the grand paved esplanade that leads to the Colonnaded Street. The monumental structures of the lower city are grouped around this sanctuary and artery. The building, which was further adorned during the Roman period, was well-constructed in stuccoed sandstone with a system of juniper-wood beams designed to protect it from earthquakes. Right: a fragment of the Roman decoration.

At the far end of the Qasr al-Bint temple, two staircases lead to a platform that held the idol of the god Dushara. The 10th-century Byzantine dictionary called the *Souda* describes this as "a black, quadrangular, aniconic stone. Its height is four feet and its width is two feet. It rests upon a golden plinth. They offer it sacrifices and pour the blood of their victims upon it. Such is their libation." In the early Christian era, the temple was used as a church. Before the date of Christmas was fixed in December, the birth of Christ, born to a virgin, was celebrated there each January 6.

Biyara mountain. Inscriptions and images of divinities indicate that in this great temple various divinities were subordinated to the primary goddess, al-'Uzza, and the edifice became the representative monument of the emerging settled community.

The Hellenization and Romanization of Petra

By the Roman period, the cities of the East had absorbed classical tastes and concepts of urban planning, including the street grid. Although the Romans could not impose a

coherent grid upon preexisting cities, they did make some districts regular, generally the areas around the grand public buildings that were erected or rebuilt during this period. In Petra, sanctuaries and markets were aligned on a street plan, but higher up on both banks of the Wadi Musa, the layout of residential areas simply followed the contours of the hills, or was at best reordered inexpensively into terraces. It is significant that the houses recently excavated in ez-Zantur do not face onto actual streets. With the exception of the straight Colonnaded Street, the routes of communication were adapted to the difficult terrain; they did not serve as elements in any master plan. These irregular caravan trails, processional routes, and messengers' footpaths had a vital function in the city system and ensured its cohesion.

Above: the theater underwent several successive enlargements and alterations. It was an important building for the city; as was often the case, it was probably used for both plays and public meetings. The stage and the back wall were richly decorated with columns and, during the Roman period, with imported marble statues.

The colonnaded main street appears in practically all Roman cities of the Near East. It was a primary instrument of urban planning, serving to unify space and to give the pedestrian the sense of a grand, coherent urban structure. At Petra, the Colonnaded Street was built (and rebuilt) during the 2d century AD along the Wadi Musa, whose course was straightened to run due east–west through the center of the basin. Throughout the late-Roman period, it was a vast commercial center and a place of social gathering, both indispensable for a city. Another major element of any Greco-Roman city was its theater. The one in Petra, constructed during the 1st century AD, was used for both secular and religious festivals.

Religious space: temples and open-air sanctuaries

Petra itself was also a sacred space. Dispersed throughout the site (somewhat unevenly), are great numbers of ruins with religious significance; these range from simple dedications to a god to great temples in the center of the city. The Qasr al-Bint, dedicated in the second half of the 1st century BC to Dushara-Zeus-Hypsistos ("the Most High") and al-'Uzza-Aphrodite, dominates a group of sanctuaries built on the facing slopes: the Temple of the Winged Lions to the north, which may have been dedicated to the same divine couple (assimilated to the Egyptian gods Isis and Osiris), and two others to the south. In the largest of these, ongoing excavations conducted by an American team from Brown University have revealed an unexpected array of semicircular tiers of seating, reminiscent of a council hall. Higher up, the freestanding column known as Zibb Far'un may be the vestige of another sanctuary. Farther from the center stood less important temples, of which incomplete architectural elements remain.

More plentiful are the rock shrines, many of which survive. The so-called High Places are the most characteristic; these are religious precincts set on the crown of a mountain, with a commanding view of the landscape. They usually comprise a

Below: the Colonnaded Street, the main street and social center of the city, follows the course of the Wadi Musa, which is visible as an open area at right. The street was rerouted several times and acquired its monumental appearance at a date not yet fixed with certainty—probably just before or after the Roman annexation in 106. It was an evenly paved roadway some 20 feet (6 meters) wide, with two rows of columns. On its south side, at left, were rows of shops. Markets and large public and religious buildings scaled the slope behind.

triclinium, a chamber rimmed with rows of benches, used for devotional banquets; a raised platform reserved for the celebrant; an altar; a pedestal for a cult object; a basin for purification; and one or more cisterns. The most spectacular of the High Places is Madhbah, overlooking the center of Petra, but there are others on many of the city's summits. Other religious shrines—mainly collections of sculpted niches—mark important natural features, such as hill crests and places where water issues forth. These include the grotto of Umm al-Biyara; Qattar ad-Deir,

Left: the great Temple of the Winged Lions, overlooking the northern bank of the Wadi Musa, was so named because of the feline decorations on its Corinthian capitals. The main section is a large altar platform bordered by twelve columns, at the center of a square *cella* surrounded by a portico intended for the ritual ceremony of walking around an idol. The stele dedicated to "the goddess of Hayyan" (page 34) was found here. The foundation of the temple has been dated to before AD 27. It was partly destroyed by earthquake in AD 363.

where water seeps along the rock face; and Sidd al-Ma'jjin, where it churns in a gorge during the flood season. Small, basic shrines, consisting of a niche bearing a Nabataean baetyl or Greco-Roman icon, were located both near residences and in deserted spots, as were simple inscriptions naming the gods and their worshipers. These little shrines were dedicated to various divinities, among whom Egyptian Isis occupied a position of importance.

Processions and ritual banquets

The majority of this accumulated religious material is located along the main roads, the caravan tracks, and the internal roadways of the city, particularly the Siq, which has some of the characteristics of a Greco-Roman Sacred Way. Roads used for pilgrimages or processions sometimes acquired a ritualistic value, and some seem to have served no other purpose than as a sanctuary.

The varying scale and locations of these sanctuaries suggest the relative importance of the cults with which

Below: on the summit of Jabal Madhbah, at the foot of the principal High Place, stand two obelisks 19 and 23 feet high (6 and 7 meters). Both monoliths were cut from the same rock—a

they were associated. The smallest cult venues—an inscription or a baetyl in a niche—may have been installed by a single individual, while a grandiose edifice such as the Qasr al-Bint was doubtless a royal commission. Shrines of middle size, such as the High Places, presented locations where a large family group or particular community—as many as several hundred people—could gather. They served as both meeting halls and temples. The triclinia, or banquet halls, were found in several contexts. Whether covered or open-air, rock-hewn or stone-built, they could be linked with sanctuaries, tombs, or residences. Strabo, quoting Athenodorus, notes that the banquet was a fundamental ritual that expressed and reinforced the solidarity of a social group. Banquets were held in honor of tutelary divinities, a deceased family member,

remarkable effort. Following an ancient Edomite tradition, they may represent a divine couple, perhaps Dushara and al-'Uzza or Allat. Opposite below: a baetyl known as an Eye Idol still bears traces of the bronze, stucco, and precious stones with which it was once decorated.

The most celebrated High Place is on the summit of Jabal Madhbah. The faithful must have gathered in the large rectangular space (at right in the upper photograph), surrounded on three sides by benches. At its center is a platform that perhaps served as a tribune or sacrificial table. To the left is a podium with an altar broad enough to accommodate a large sacrificial animal, such as a camel. This is reached by a stairway, and was reserved for officiating priests. A carved mortise at the top of the altar may once have held a portable icon. Nearby are a circular basin, also reached by a stair, with a rectangular cistern before it. One can imagine the grand processions up the pathways and flights of stairs to this high spot. Lower left and right: several of these paths are lined with niches, some containing sculptures of baetyls, some empty, though they may once have held statues.

or an ancestor. This tradition is also found in Rome.

Some of the High Places seem to preside over a particular district of the city. Were they the residue of earlier land partitions among some of the social or tribal groups? In Palmyra, each of the major sanctuaries is directly associated with one or several tribes, who are named in inscriptions. Unfortunately, in Petra, inscriptions in the sanctuaries and tombs remain rare. Nonetheless, it is through these inscriptions that archaeologists are able to identify a necropolis as belonging to a particular family or group of families. One such is the Turkmaniyya Tomb, whose monumental and detailed Nabataean inscription we have already noted.

The architecture of the temples and their decoration

Nabataean temple architecture, like many other aspects of the culture, reflects an amalgam of indigenous and acquired traits. A number of temples have an *adyton,* a

Above: the Soldier's Triclinium is a rock-cut banquet hall connected with the Tomb of the Roman Soldier. It lies west of the theater, near the Wadi Farasa, and is the room sketched by Laborde on page 16. Banquet halls are quite varied: some have three tiers of benches (a triclinium), others two tiers (a biclinium), or a single semicircular one (stibadium). They have been found in many Roman cities, sometimes even in residential areas, and are linked to funerary rituals or divinity cults.

detached inner sanctum at the far end of the building. This indicates that a ritual ceremony, common to many ancient Oriental cults, was practiced in which worshipers walked around a baetyl that had been placed upon a pedestal in this space.

Left: this sketch attempts a reconstruction of the funerary complex of the Tomb and Triclinium of the Roman Soldier, which lies in the narrow gorge of the Wadi Farasa. A courtyard of colonnaded porticos fills the ravine, at one end of which, at left, is the entrance to the rock-cut triclinium. Facing this, at right, is the tomb's facade; in its central niche is the statue from which it takes its name. Supplementary structures such as the grand porticos and some decorative elements of the facade signaled the owners' importance or that of their ancestor. The court also had a utilitarian purpose; unfortunately, virtually nothing of it remains. One of the rare tomb inscriptions preserved at Petra mentions an orchard attached to a tomb. It is possible that the Garden Temple complex, located just beyond the Tomb of the Roman Soldier, belonged to the same group of monuments.

Nonetheless, many other architectural elements of temples reflect Hellenistic and Roman style. The Nabataeans borrowed the use of the engaged or blind colonnade in the interior of a building from their neighbors, as can be seen in the Temple of the Winged Lions. Sometimes they used it in the facade, as in the Qasr al-Bint, with either a real or false pediment, and a portico enclosing a courtyard or sheltering annexes.

They were above all inspired by Hellenistic architectural grammar, which they adapted freely—the three classical architectural orders, Doric, Ionic, and Corinthian, appear throughout Petra's temples and tombs—and by Hellenistic decorative motifs, to which they added their inherited repertoire of ancient Near Eastern motifs.

Ultimately, the models for temples, shrines, and tombs come from Alexandria, on the Mediterranean

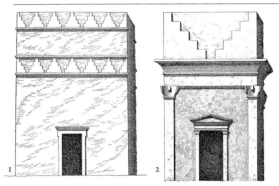

coast of Egypt. This Hellenistic Greek city was a major destination of the caravan trade and undoubtedly Nabataea's primary commercial and cultural partner. Recent archaeological discoveries there confirm the connection: a two-pronged column style known as the "Nabataean" capital has been found there; this is a capital whose silhouette is based upon the Corinthian, but whose surface is left smooth so as to be stuccoed or painted. Such capitals are found throughout Nabataea. It is possible that the Nabataean kings brought architects and sculptors from Alexandria to work on their great construction projects, such as the Qasr al-Bint, and that these artisans remained and founded a local school, where they handed down favored architectural forms at least through the 2nd century AD.

The tombs and their facades

It is Petra's funerary architecture, most famous in its rock-hewn form, that best reflects this dual cultural identity, Eastern and Hellenistic. Interest has focused on the facades that mark the entry to a funerary chamber excavated directly into the rock. These can be understood as a monumental form of the *nefesh,* an erect stele that indicates the presence of a deceased, just as a baetyl indicates the presence of a divinity. The facade shows the importance of the deceased and of his or her family. Occasionally, porticos or orchards abutted the tombs, and often banquet halls, where families gathered for funeral ceremonies and commemorative feasts.

Above: five Eastern-style facade types. From left to right: 1) a tower tomb, crowned by two rows of merlons, or corbiesteps; 2) a proto–Hegra-type tomb, with angled and stepped demimerlons, an Egyptian cavetto cornice, and a doorway flanked by two pilasters; 3) a Hegra-type tomb, which has a double entablature; 4) and 5) Hegra-type tombs whose double entablature is adorned with dwarf pilasters. The sixth example is a tomb facade in the classical (Hellenistic) style, with triangular pediment, double pilasters, an arch above the door, and the repeated ornamental motif of an urn.

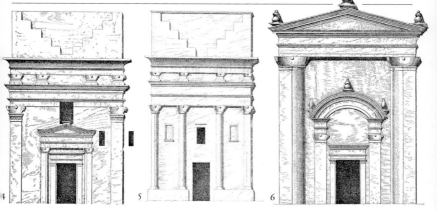

Two facade types are distinguishable by their decorations; one is in the Eastern tradition, the other Hellenistic. The latter form was used in the most spectacular royal monuments, such as the famous El Khazneh and ad-Deir, and other great tombs at the foot of al-Khubtha. Facades in the Eastern tradition are not necessarily older than the Hellenistic ones. They tended to be simpler and less ornate, with a square silhouette, rather than a triangular entablature, and were probably less costly. Some Oriental-style facades had a Hellenistic-style doorway, called a *naïskos,* shaped like a small Greco-Roman temple entrance. There are also more simple designs, such as cube and arch tombs.

A Nabataean style?

This dual inspiration can also be seen in Nabataean crafts. A distinctive ceramicware began to be made in the 1st century BC, replacing the commonplace local pottery. It is immediately recognizable by its delicacy and high quality, the color of its clay, and its painted-leaf decorations and other motifs. It is in the

Below: the Petra version of a Greco-Roman Corinthian capital retains the classical profile, but is smooth and unadorned; it was a symbol of Nabataean power.

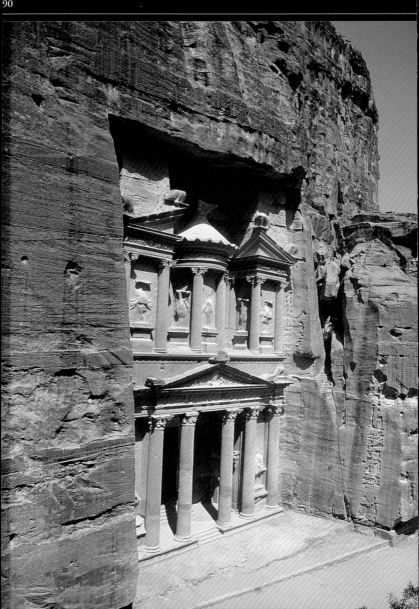

The glory of Petra

Preceding pages: some of the most famous funerary monuments of Petra. Page 86: ad-Deir, the so-called Monastery, whose imposing facade is 148 feet (45 meters) wide by 138 feet (42 meters) tall. It was undoubtedly linked to a funerary cult, perhaps that of the deified King Obodas I. Page 87: the great Urn Tomb, a Doric-style burial chamber cut into the cliffs of al-Khubtha, one of several with Hellenistic facades that belonged to princes or nobles. In AD 447 this was converted into a church. Page 88: the Renaissance Tomb in the Wadi Farasa area. Some scholars have dated it to the 2d century BC. Page 89: the Obelisk Tomb, which stands at the entrance to the Siq gorge, is named for its four "obelisks"—in reality a type of pyramid that indicated the presence of the deceased, as did a statue placed in the niche above the door. Opposite: the facade of the royal tomb of El Khazneh. This page, above left: a Hellenistic-style Corinthian capital from the peristyle of El Khazneh; above right: a detail of the blind rotunda, or *tholos,* of its facade, with a central figure of Isis-Tyche, holding a cornucopia. Below: a view within the peristyle entrance of El Khazneh, looking toward the door to a side room.

decorations, more than the shapes, that the link to an Eastern style may be seen. Typological classifications and chronological sequencing conducted at numerous sites show that the production of these ceramics continued long after the Roman annexation of Nabataea in AD 106. They are found throughout the realm itself and along the full length of its trade routes; examples have been unearthed as far away as Bosra. Potters' workshops have also been excavated at several distant sites— for example, in the Negev—proving that the manufacture of these ceramics was not limited to the metropolis. They have frequently been found together with imported wares—lamps from Alexandria, Greece, and southern Italy; vases imported from all over— and local imitations of these.

Excavations have also produced an abundance of terra-cotta and bronze statuettes of animals, small human figures, and occasionally gods; some of these were imported from Alexandria, but most were made locally. Alexandrian influence is also visible in paintings and stucco decorations. There are surviving frescos at Petra, and some large buildings still preserve fragments of their stucco ornamentation. These are characterized by a typically Alexandrian motif of profuse foliage, rich with a variety of birds and small winged cupids and other fabulous creatures.

Left: the type of clay used in this goblet, as well as the radiating-leaf motif of its painted decoration, is characteristic of Nabataean ceramics. Such ceramics have been classified according to type and period; the resulting data reveal that they were produced not only at Petra, but throughout Nabataea, and continued to be made well after it became a Roman province.

The same influence can also be seen in the local stone sculpture, the richest examples of which are found in reliefs on Petra's principal monuments and at the twin sites of Khirbet Tannur and Khirbet edh-Dharih. Such relief sculptures are rarely found beyond southern Jordan. The sculpture of the Hauran, for example, is related to other provincial currents of Greco-Roman art. Although the dating is highly disputed, the common ancestry of these works, however eclectic, remains clear. They were certainly inspired by classical models, but the local artists who made them interpreted many details in their own manner. Oriental characteristics appear in the handling of draperies and the faces of some figures; the late-Roman period of Egyptian art (3d century AD and after) sometimes recalls these. However, some busts found at Petra—a bit more refined and probably of Alexandrian provenance—are much closer to the earlier style of the Hellenistic period in Egypt. Some bronze and marble statues discovered in the city were almost certainly imported from Alexandria.

During the Roman imperial period, Greco-Roman models came into general use in Petra, and the few "local" characteristics that can be identified in the later architecture and the Byzantine-era mosaics no longer owed much to Nabataean origins.

Above: this fine ornamental relief of Eros with a winged lion, found at Petra, belongs to a series of sculptures whose source is probably Alexandrian. Keynotes of Hellenistic style are a graceful sense of movement, a taste for variety of forms, and delicate ornamentation, despite an almost heraldic formal composition. Opposite: this limestone head, which may depict a priest, blends classical characteristics with Eastern influences. Some of the features look Greco-Roman, while others, such as the headdress and the stylized curls of the beard, recall the Parthian sculptures of Hatra, in Iraq. It is from an unknown Jordanian site, possibly Petra.

Petra after the Nabataeans

Beginning in the imperial period, the ancient Nabataean nucleus of the population gradually merged with Arabs of other origins. The original features that marked the art of this community—the taste for rock-hewn facades, the idiosyncratic architectural decorations, the ceramics— slowly grew less distinctive, well before the Nabataeans themselves disappeared as a separate people. In the Byzantine era, Petra was promoted to the rank of metropolis of the province and see of the Christian bishopric, and continued to be a fairly active city, with flourishing monasteries. Important buildings were built (the churches, for example), some decorated with exquisitely fine mosaics. However, due to a series of earthquakes, especially one in the 8th century, construction seems to have come to a halt there earlier than it did in regions farther to the north.

We know little about Petra between the 7th and 10th centuries. By the Middle Ages, it may have been virtually deserted. We know that in the 12th century, one of the Crusader kings of Jerusalem, Baldwin I or II, built a castle at al-Wuʿeira, in the Valley of Moses. Few medieval documents refer to the city, but a confused memory of its ancient rank as the capital of a far-reaching kingdom lived on. Oddly, traces of its old Aramaic and Nabataean name, Arken or Reqem, meaning "the Multicolored," survived. In 1217, a German pilgrim named Thetmar passed very close to a place he called "Archim, formerly the metropolis of the Arabs." The Arab chronicler Numeiri (1279–1332) gives a short description of the site as it was when the Mamluk Sultan Baybars I of Egypt and Syria saw it in 1276. He mentions the tomb of Aaron, the ruins of a fort, and the "marvelous" ornate houses cut into the cliffs, but he does not name it. Neither writer says anything of its inhabitants. The Nabataeans themselves, and the Greco-Latin name Petra, remained lost until the rediscovery of the city by the first Western travelers of the 19th century.

The enthusiasm aroused by this discovery has not faded, and the work of exploration and recovery is nowhere near to being finished. Nearly two hundred

The Corinthian Tomb has eroded badly; weather and time have stripped its delicate sandstone. Little by little, the most exposed facades in Petra are dissolving.

years of research, in fact, have raised more questions than answers. New avenues of investigation emerge daily. Most of the city still remains to be excavated and the civilization of Nabataea finally revealed.

Overleaf: El Khazneh, seen from the air.

DOCUMENTS

"Petra…the name is said to come from the Greek word for stone, or rock, since the city itself was hollowed out of the rock. But it may just as well have come from the Arabic *batara,* meaning to cut or hew, since the city was actually carved from rock…perhaps this is even the better etymology, since this was a place cut off from the rest of the world."

Nabil Naoum,
Le Château de la princesse (*The Castle of the Princess*),
from *Pétra: Le Dit des pierres* (*Petra: The Stones Speak*),
edited by Philippe Cardinal, 1993

Nabataea

From the time when they first settled in the biblical land of Edom, the Nabataeans extended their territory. A successful monarchy forged a cohesive empire, despite its fluid borders. The sites of Nabataea reveal both diversity and common elements, including an adroit adaptation of difficult terrain. Petra itself, however, is unique.

Sabra

Near Petra lies the site of Sabra, or el Sabrah, notable for its beauty.

The distant suburb of el Sabrah appears to have been quite a sizeable town in its own right. It enjoyed the amenity of a neat, small theatre along prescribed classical lines—no doubt Roman—and there are the remains of what looked like large barrack buildings, perhaps for a garrison defending the southern approaches to the city. We know little about the Nabatean army, although it is certain that they must have maintained a military establishment of certain size to protect the routes under their control. There is ample evidence of this in many inscriptions at Hegra (Medain Saleh) and at other Nabatean sites.

The theater of Sabra, south of Petra, in an engraving based on an 1830 drawing by Léon de Laborde.

What form this establishment took is open to question but it is probable that the Nabateans, who were almost pathologically addicted to trade, would have tolerated better some form of Territorial Army or Ever-Ready force, than a full-scale standing army. This quickly mobilised reserve would have been able to support the professional force. The barracks at el Sabrah may, of course, be Roman, in which case they are almost sure to be for military use.

It must, however, not be forgotten that the hillsides about el Sabrah are riddled with mines. There is a view that the Edomites were really a mining and metallurgical people whose main sphere of activity lay further to the north...

Until, however, el Sabrah has been excavated it is impossible to say whether the minerals there were exploited by the Edomites. There is no evidence of the Nabateans having been particularly inclined to extractive metallurgy but this does not mean that mining was not carried out. El Sabrah might have been a mining and industrial suburb of Petra complete with its own facilities and civic life, and the "barracks" might be explained as having provided housing for the large number of expatriate workers needed to operate the mines, and presumably the smelters.

Iain Browning,
Petra, 1973

Wadi Sabra

The water sources in the area around Petra played an essential role in the development of the city.

The southern extremity of the Petra district is the Sabra valley, which runs down from the southern side of the south watershed between two outlying parallel ridges of sandstone until, meeting a projection of the Cretaceous ridge, it is diverted to the west and runs down into Wadi Araba round the southern flank of Mount Hor. The only importance of this valley, which is of some width, is that it has a perennial spring and rivulet about a mile below the watershed, and it was for that reason occupied in Roman times by a military outpost for the defense of Petra against attack from the south. Close by the spring there is a mass of tumbled masonry, with occasional broken pillars and capitals marking the site of the barracks and other buildings of the Roman garrison, while the mouth of a ravine issuing from the hillside on the left bank of the Wadi was ingeniously made by the garrison to serve the purposes of a theatre—its seats being carved out of the sloping sandstone rock-face, while the bed of the ravine itself, intervening between the two wings of the theatre, was bridged by masonry seats built over a drain designed to carry off the water descending the ravine into the main Wadi. The Sabra outpost lies at an elevation of about 2,540 feet above sea-level, and is thus the lowest of the Petra localities. An abundant supply of excellent water and the amenities of the theatre doubtless attracted a small colony of merchants in addition to the garrison of the place, and we may conjecture that the locality also served as a winter-resort for inhabitants of the capital desiring a change of air or a holiday. The bed of the valley down-stream of the spring is spread over with a thick covering of luxuriant vegetation, through which the (apparently) perennial stream runs for a considerable distance. The containing ridges of Wadi

Sabra constitute, as has been suggested above, a natural continuation of the ruddy sandstone strata of the eastern ridge, which runs down from the north to Jabal Manza at the head of the valley and thence bifurcates.

Sir Alexander B. W. Kennedy,
Petra: Its History and Monuments,
1925

The approaches to Petra

Petra is famed for the romantic drama of its hidden site. Adding to its allure is the spectacular landscape surrounding it, which has inspired much fine descriptive writing.

The view of Petra from just above Alji village, particularly at dawn before the rays of the rising sun have reached the pinnacled summits of the sandstone sierra, is one of infinite, ineffable charm. The soft hues of the rose-tinted rock-barrier before one will later in the day harden into too crude outlines of light and shadow, but at that hour they float with an appearance of unreality like a veil before the mysteries one has dared to approach. Few scenes in Nature can more adequately represent that fairyland which is man's dream-picture of perfection. That scene does, indeed, approach perfection, creating as it does in the beholder a sense of awe and mystery without which the climax of that glimpse of the Khazna temple [the tomb of El Khazneh]—again before the sun has reached its face or when the moon is upon it—through the darkling walls of the Siq gorge, should not be approached. It is, indeed, well worth the while of the visitor to arrange the time and manner of his approach to Petra in such a way as to secure the most striking effect upon his senses, but material

difficulties of travel—perhaps one should say material facilities now that the motor-car has substantially shortened the journey from the railway—may render this not always feasible. It so happens, however, that the easiest approach to Petra under modern conditions—it was also the regular approach to it for tourists before the War, though then toilsome and laborious—enjoys the advantage of bringing the visitor with thrilling abruptness to the very verge of the mountain-crest, below which, far below, Petra lies exposed to view in all its glory and, more than Petra, the abyss of the Rift Valley beyond, the summits of distant Midian and the haze-bound uplands of Palestine towards Sinai. Those who have driven by car from Anaiza station across the plain and along the valley of Ain Najal and up through the treeless forest of al Hisha with the elusive horizon of al Shara ever before them—seemingly impossible to reach as ridge succeeds to ridge—and have come suddenly without warning at Ras al Khaur to the edge of that vast chasm with its tossing sea of ruddy peaks below and have looked down on Petra, will never forget that scene. It is one that defies the photographer and cannot be described...

Sir Alexander B. W. Kennedy,
Petra: Its History and Monuments,
1925

Khirbet Tannur

On the northern boundary of what was once the land of Edom lie the ruins of two Nabataean sanctuaries. Built on the great north–south trade route called the King's Highway they were prosperous and have yielded rich archaeological finds, including much sculpture. Recent excavations in the region have found reliefs representing

N abataean ruins at Qasrawet, a town strategically placed in a commanding commercial location at the border of Egypt.

Hellenistic divinities, including figures of Victory, Hermes, and the Dioscuri.

Between the high cliffs at its northern border and the string of jagged massifs to the south, the wadi of al-Hasa is squeezed between the alluvial deposits carried by its left-bank tributaries. Standing alone in the valley, a steep mound rises to 700 meters [2,300 feet] near the confluence of the wadi of al-Hasa and of La'ban that flows 400 meters [1,300 feet] below.

Here on this high plateau the Nabataeans built their remarkable sanctuary. Excavated in 1937 by Nelson Glueck, the Tannur sanctuary takes up almost the entire top of the mound. It is made up of a double court with an east–west orientation, the western half slightly higher than the eastern one, where the entrance is situated. The banquet halls and sacristies—three on

each side—open from the northern and southern sides of the two courts. Before the eastern court, in the northeast corner of the sanctuary, there is another triclinium.

Maurice Sartre,
Inscriptions de la Jordanie
(*Inscriptions of Jordan*), vol. 4,
in *Inscriptions grecques et latines de la Syrie*
(*Greek and Latin Inscriptions in Syria*), vol. 21, 1993

Wadi Rum

Rum, or Iram, lies to the south of Petra, on the route that leads to the port cities of the Red Sea.

Wadi Rum—known as Iram in Nabataean texts that were found at the site, as well as among Arab writers in the Middle Ages—was the site of one of the most famous Nabataean sanctuaries. It continued as a hub of activity long after the region became independent. It appears as a wide, dry, and very flat valley, running north to south and bordered by two high cliffs, so steep that they almost form right angles…The archaeological record includes two types of religious complexes. In the southwest corner of a thrust fault, and dominating the valley for several dozen meters, lies the rock sanctuary of [the goddess] Allat, chosen as a site because of the presence there of the Ain Shallalah spring. At the foot of the cliff—literally—rose a temple, also most likely dedicated to Allat, and a small settlement.

Both were first discovered in 1931 by George Horsfield and were jointly explored between 1932 and 1934 by the inventor and by Father Raphaël Savignac. Excavations of the temple below were later undertaken by Diana Kirkbride. After a long hiatus, the project was recently continued, and the exploration has spread to the surrounding area, where sites of Nabataean and Thamoudene graffiti had been found, notably at Rizqeh, south of Rum.

Maurice Sartre,
Inscriptions de la Jordanie
(*Inscriptions of Jordan*), vol. 4

Bosra, the second capital

Beginning in the Hellenistic era, the Nabataeans occupied what is now southern Syria, especially the southern part of the massif of the Hauran and the fertile region of Salkhad and Bosra. Under the Romans, Bosra became the capital of the province of Arabia.

The second capital of the Nabataean realm, Bosra, lay at the hub of a rich, grain-producing agricultural zone, and brought new resources to the dynasty. The discovery of painted Nabataean ceramicware throughout the city suggests that the population was Nabataean, as do the inscriptions referring to the cult of Dushara and Allat.

In the mid-1st century AD, the Nabataeans redeveloped the city by creating a new district, with a different street orientation, to the east of the existing town. The authorities were eager to put their stamp on this venture and built a monumental arch, adorned with characteristic Nabataean horned capitals, at the end of the main east–west thoroughfare, marking the passage from the old city to the new.

In the center of this district was a group of monumental buildings, undoubtedly a sanctuary, in the form of a great court surrounded by porticos. This was built over sometime between the 4th and 5th centuries by a large cathedral with a central floor plan.

Roman coins show a *motab*, a kind of podium, with baetyls that may be from this sanctuary, perhaps dedicated to Dushara. Fragments of stone architectural ornament, found at the center of the city and to the east, attest to the presence of other buildings of this period.

Jean-Marie Dentzer

International trade

Nabataean culture was shaped by trade, and the realm's wealth fluctuated with its fortunes in the international markets.

The nature and number of Nabataean temples bear a direct relationship to the prosperity enjoyed by the Nabataean kingdom, particularly from the second century BC to the second century AD…
Much of the merchandise of the

Orient passed through the hands of the Nabataeans, bringing them great revenue. It was brought in part by caravan across the emptiness of Arabia from the port of Gerrha on the west side of the Persian Gulf of Aqabah, which is the eastern arm of the Red Sea. From there it was shipped by boat or sent overland by caravan northward to Nabataean Aila on the northeastern rim of the gulf. The next leg of the journey was the much-traveled route to the great distribution center of Petra, to which also a direct overland route led from the important Nabataean center of Meda'in Saleh in Arabia. From Petra, in turn, the precious goods flowed to Syria, Palestine, Egypt and Europe, carried by beast or boat as the case might be.

The trans-Arabian traffic made use of the bases of Hail, Jauf, Teima, Tebuk, Khaiber and Dedan, in addition to Meda'in Saleh. And one of the main caravan routes from Petra led across the Negev and Sinai "to Rhinocolura…and thence to other nations…," according to the Greek geographer, Strabo, who wrote about the Nabataeans at the beginning of the first century AD. Ships laden with Nabataean merchandise set forth then from the port of Rhinocolura, modern el-Arish on the Mediterranean coast of Sinai, or from Gaza or Ascalon in Palestine, to ply the eastern Mediterranean and touch North African or European ports. A Graeco-Nabataean inscription has been discovered on the island of Rhodes, and a Nabataean sanctuary probably existed at one of the chief ports of call in Italy, namely, at Puteoli, a few miles west of Naples.

Caravan stations developed into flourishing towns as a result of the progressive improvement of the Nabataean economy, with each of them becoming graced, in the course of time, with a temple of its own. The press of population growth that accompanied increasing prosperity forced the Nabataeans intensively to occupy even such marginal lands as the Negev and Sinai, in addition to the fertile areas of former Edom and Moab. It required unremitting effort and infinite ingenuity for them to secure the necessary water and food supplies for the amazingly large number of their desert settlements. Their achievements surpassed the efforts of any of their predecessors. They found it possible to restore and considerably to enlarge the possibilities of settlement in the semi-arid Negev by improving the methods and intensifying the conservation measures that the Judaeans had employed there before them. Whatever the Nabataeans touched, from Arabia to Syria and Sinai, seemed to flourish under their vigorous and enlightened direction.

The brilliant civilization they fashioned through much commerce, some industry and intensive agriculture and animal husbandry, commands admiration even when seen in its ruins. So powerful was the momentum of their creativity, that some of their finest buildings were erected after the structure of their state had collapsed. Indeed, the impact of its conquest by Trajan in AD 106/107 and its incorporation into the Provincia Arabia of Roman rule was hardly noticed at first. Gradually, however, the strength of the Nabataean economy ebbed as the result of changes initiated by the new masters.

Nelson Glueck,
Deities and Dolphins, 1965

Petra after the Nabataeans

Under the last rulers of Nabataea, Petra suffered from the decline in caravan traffic. Nonetheless, its prestige as an ancient royal capital won it the title "metropolis." In the late Roman imperial and early Christian periods, it became a regional administrative and religious center. Yet despite the continuing development of the surrounding areas, the city was eventually abandoned.

N abataean clay oil lamps found at Petra.

The Byzantine era

Petra became largely Christian in the last centuries of the Roman Empire. Yet pagan worship endured until quite late, and Islam took hold soon after it faded.

Early in the 4th century the Emperor Diocletian reorganized the administration of the entire Roman Empire. As far as the Arabian territories were concerned, in the north Bostra [Bosra] remained capital of a revised Province of Arabia; the south, including Petra, eventually became known as Palaestina Tertia, a division of the Province of Palestine.

In 330 the Emperor Constantine the Great transferred the capital of the Roman Empire to the Greek city of Byzantium [now Istanbul]…From being a persecuted religion, Christianity now became the most favoured, and by the end of the 4th century it had become institutionalized as the state religion throughout both eastern and western parts of the Empire.

Petra had already had its Christian martyrs in the persecutions of Diocletian. These thought-provoking examples must have had the de-Christianizing effect Diocletian desired, for very soon afterwards the Christian chronicler Eusebius thundered against Petra for being "filled with superstitious men, who have sunk in diabolical error." He was clearly exaggerating, for churches were already being built there…

Pagan worship continued in Petra side by side with Christianity—a state of affairs that a certain mobster monk called Bar Sauma felt called upon to rectify. He and forty brother monks, who were travelling about the Empire destroying pagan temples, arrived in Petra in 423 to find the gates shut fast against them. Their demands to be let in, accompanied by threats of attack and conflagration if they were not, coincided with a rainstorm of such intensity that part of the city wall was broken and the godly gang poured in. The whole episode was deemed to be of truly miraculous significance as there had been an unbroken drought for four years, and the impressed pagan priests duly converted to Christianity.

Over the following century or so, bishops from Petra took part in the various Councils of the Church, convened to discuss the series of doctrinal disagreements which followed the Arian controversy with dizzying frequency. Petra also seems to have become a place of exile for troublous or heretical priests, prelates or prominent laymen who failed to agree either with the Emperor or with the decisions of these Councils. The most famous such exile—according to one contemporary document—was Nestorius, author of the Nestorian heresy which was condemned at the Council of Ephesus in 431…

On 9 July 551 a…devastating earthquake reduced most of what remained of Petra to heaps of rubble. It was never rebuilt, and soon the bishops departed and all records came to an end. In this state of tumbled decay Petra had little to lose in accepting the new Islamic power that replaced the Byzantines in the region in 633. It had little to offer, either, and became a forgotten backwater of the Arab and Islamic world.

The silence that again descended on Petra was broken by the arrival of the Crusaders in the early 12th century. Some Christian monks, who still inhabited the Monastery of St Aaron on Jabal Haroun, the highest mountain in the Petra area, asked King Baldwin I of Jerusalem for help as they were under threat from Saracen raiders on the ancient trade route. Answering this *cri de coeur,* Baldwin realized the value of this area east of the rift valley, and he decided to establish there the district of Oultre Jourdain, an outpost of the Kingdom of Jerusalem. The Bedouin of the area resisted their arrival, and were punished by being smoked out of the caves in which they lived.

To defend their new territory, the Crusaders built a string of fortresses in the eastern mountains. Here, in this area that they called Li Vaux Moise,…the largest and strongest was the castle now called al-Wu'eira just outside Petra. A smaller fort was built on al-Habees, a high point in the heart of the ancient city, to complete their signalling sight-line to Jerusalem. Li Vaux Moise was abandoned in 1189, the last of the eastern fortresses to surrender to Salah ad-Din (Saladin), and the Crusaders withdrew to the Mediterranean.

Over the long span of the centuries that followed, the Bedouin of Petra must have gone about their herding and tilling, inhabiting the caves and tombs of the Nabataeans during the cold winter months, and moving to higher pastures in the long hot season…

In the west, Petra all but disappeared from minds and maps alike, and was known only to scholars from a few tantalizing references by Greek, Roman, Byzantine and Crusader authors.

Jane Taylor,
Petra, 1995

The Byzantine church

This site has splendid mosaics.

In 1973 the American archaeologist Dr Kenneth W. Russell noticed the outline of an apse on a slope north of the Colonnaded Street. When he returned in April 1990 to do a formal recording of the site, he concluded that the ruins were of a large Byzantine church which, from the considerable quantities of small glass tesserae that lay scattered on the surface, must have been richly decorated with mosaics on its walls and ceilings. Any church that had wall and ceiling mosaics would also have had the more common floor mosaics, executed with larger stone tesserae.

Excavation of the site…revealed a triple-apsed church, of the 6th century or possibly earlier, with an atrium to the west. It had been badly damaged by fire, apparently quite soon after it was built, and its destruction may have been completed by the earthquake of 551.

Handsome mosaic floors were found covering both side aisles, with geometrical designs and lively depictions of human figures, birds and animals. Despite the thousands of tesserae from wall and ceiling mosaics, there are insufficient large fragments to give any idea of the designs. The central nave was originally paved with marble, interspersed with strips of local red sandstone, but the marble disappeared long before the church filled with driftsand. Fortunately, other pieces of marble remained in place, including colonnettes, three altars, and some carved marble panels from a chancel screen which had been broken into many pieces by early treasure hunters. Painstaking restoration has revealed a quality of carving which is among the finest so far found in Jordan.

Although the church is large enough to have been a cathedral, there is no evidence that this was its function. But any church that had such care and expense lavished on it, in a city of the importance of Petra, must have been of considerable significance.

Jane Taylor,
Petra, 1995

An ancient archive

Papyrus scrolls of the Byzantine era have been found at Petra, offering precious insights into life in the 6th century.

In the church discovered on the peak of Jabal Qabr Jume'an, north of the Colonnaded Street, the ACOR [American Center for Oriental Research (Amman)] excavations in December 1993 found a pile of carbonized papyrus scrolls. One hundred fifty-two scrolls or fragments have been identified, including 42 that preserve a continuous text. They were stored on shelves in an annex located at the northeast corner of the church. These were private archives dated mostly between 528 and 582, in which the same names recur regularly. They can be attributed to the family of Theodorus, son of Obodianus, who was archdeacon of the church, which explains why they had been deposited there. Through the marriage of young Theodorus to Stephanous, the family formed an alliance with another, that of Bassus, with whom it quickly came into conflict over the dowry. The settlement of this dispute is the subject of some of the documents. Most of the texts are wills, contracts regulating mortgages, loans, and gifts following a death, or concerning the possession, acquisition, or sale of property (including fields, vineyards, orchards, houses with fruit gardens in Petra and in a neighboring village, stables, and slaves). There is little mention of herding and livestock, and none of caravan trade.

Three brothers were the principal

landholders, owning an area estimated at 120 *jugera* (more than 74 acres, or 30 hectares). Their land was surrounded by the fields of other family members, totaling more than 200 *jugera* (117 acres, or 47 hectares). One document concerns a gift made by a dying man who called together his friends and selected two of them to administer his lands. They agreed to provide for his mother's needs until her death; at that date, the remainder of the property was to go to a church identified by name and to a poorhouse associated with it. This a rare allusion to the life of the church, with references to the "lighting of candles," the forgiveness of sins, and the "most holy and venerated glorious Holy Mother of God, forever virgin."

Although the texts are in Greek, these descendants of the Nabataeans maintained an Arab culture. Place names designating rural districts, fields, orchards, and houses are Arabic, *baith* or *darath,* transcribed into Greek.

These documents show that in the 6th century Petra was still going about its business as an organized city.

Jean-Marie Dentzer

The Crusades

Unlike many parts of Arabia, Petra did not flourish under the Muslim Umayyad rulers of the 7th and 8th centuries. It was crushed by the great earthquake of 747 and never recovered. Despite its strategic value, which led the Frankish Crusaders of Oultre Jourdain ("beyond the Jordan River") to build several forts there, it vanished from all but a few, rare medieval documents.

The Crusaders occupied the valley of the Wadi Musa, called in old French "li Vaux Moise," from 1116 to 1189, and have left fortresses at al-Wu'eira and al-Habis,

apparently without ever having recognized the site of Petra. However, [the 1st-century historian] Flavius Josephus, in his *Antiquities of the Jews,* declares that "the summit that Aaron climbed looked over Petra, once known as Arken."

In 1217, Thetmar mentions in his *Peregrinatio in Terra Sancta* (*Pilgrimage to the Holy Land,* 15:10) that on his right is Archim (which corresponds to the name Raqmu), the ancient metropolis of the Nabataeans.

The Arab chronicler Numeiri, narrating the voyage of Sultan Baybars [I] from Cairo to Kerak in 1276, refers to Petra...

"At dawn [the sultan] climbed the mountain, which was enormous, crossed by jagged passes formed of soft stone resembling conglomerate sand, with colors that changed from red to blue and white. Then he went through some gorges in the mountain just wide enough for one man at a time on horseback, where there are paths in the form of stone stairs. The tomb of Aaron, prophet of Allah, brother of Moses, peace be on both of them, is found to the traveler's left as he faces Syria...

"There are excavations in the mountain in magnificent shapes, dwellings decorated with columns and equipped with doors; the fronts of these houses are adorned with sculpture cut into the stone with a chisel, all engraved with images and shapes. They are on the scale of the dwellings of the people of today. Inside are vaulted chambers, benches facing one another, treasuries, and harems."

Fawzi Zayadine,
"Pétra et le royaume des Nabatéens"
("Petra and the Kingdom
of the Nabataeans"),
in *Les Dossiers d'archéologie* 163,
September 1991

An enduring fascination

The rediscovery of Petra during the height of the Romantic movement inspired an outpouring of prose. Some authors turned to philosophical musings, while others preferred the picturesque. Even in more recent writings we may discover certain enduring themes: the sense of alienation in a harsh, majestic landscape of barren rock; the solitude, both distressing and appealing, of the desert; and the feeling of nostalgia as the time draws near to depart from so bewitching a place.

Petra through Jordanian eyes

Dazzled as Europeans are by Petra, writers born in the region have a particular understanding of it. Here, a modern Jordanian novelist and playwright describes his response to the city.

At last Petra appeared on the horizon, but she was still not present as an emotion. My entry into the city was a kind of violence, but I did not really penetrate to her heart.

The city had begun to emerge from the heart of the rock; she devoted herself to all activities except to that of the heart; she was a head filled with impetuous dreams, above an ardent body of rosy shades that was attentive to the comings and goings of time, to the broken lances on every side...

As for the heart, it remained hidden, and its suffering was invisible...

"Why did Petra vanish?"

I answered softly:

"She didn't vanish, O stranger; she is hidden."

"Don't call me stranger...I shall enter into communion with her."

I shook my head pityingly. We remained silent until the sun, reaching its zenith, merged our two shadows; I began to feel friendly toward him, and this time I spoke first:

"What interests you about Petra? Why did you come from the ends of the earth, O stranger, to die far from your grave?"

He answered sadly:

"One never dies far from one's grave; every man carries his tomb within him, and what happens is that he enfolds himself within it; there is no external death; every death is interior, and death is easy, like living."

For the first time, I agreed with what he was saying…

Jamal Abu Hamdan,
Alternances de la veille et du rêve
(*Alternations between Waking and Dream*), 1992,
from *Pétra: Le Dit des pierres*
(*Petra: The Stones Speak*),
edited by Philippe Cardinal, 1993

An Iraqi poet of Palestinian origin, on the other hand, imagines the Petra of the living.

"The rock, the rock! Every marvelous thing is made of rock. With what skill, what patience and love, they have carved these roses of stone!…

Look! How marvelous are these abstract shapes that nature has sculpted through the ages! If only we could do the same! To sculpt in the rock that time has worked with its hands, probing to the heart of its mystery and its essence!

Then I imagined a crowd of people filling the wide space between the two mountains, this space that originally had been occupied by the squares and marketplaces of the city. Shaqilat, too, looked at them, with an expression of infinite tenderness, spreading his blessings on them, whatever might be their activities. There were sellers and buyers there, laborers and artisans, priests, thieves, young scoundrels. There were officials and farmers, blacksmiths, soldiers, potters, beggars. There were honest people and liars, the proud and the flatterers, painters, sculptors, poets who addressed compliments to passers-by, in vain. There were children laughing and crying, fathers and mothers bearing baskets of fruit and vegetables uncomplainingly—or, if they complained, they did so while sighing and begging help of the sister of Allat, whose heavenly silhouette rose up on the threshold of her imposing palace of rock.

Jabra Ibrahim Jabra,
Le Rendez-vous, (*The Meeting*), 1992,
from *Pétra: Le Dit des pierres* (*Petra: The Stones Speak*),
edited by Philippe Cardinal, 1993

Petra

This famous poem was written by an Englishman who never saw the city.

It seems no work of Man's creative hand,
By labor wrought as wavering fancy planned;
But from the rock as if by magic grown,
Eternal, silent, beautiful, alone!
Not virgin-white like that old Doric shrine,
Where erst Athena held her rites divine;
Not saintly-grey, like many a minster fane,
That crowns the hill and consecrates the plane;
But rose-red as if the blush of dawn
That first beheld them were not yet withdrawn;
The hues of youth upon a brown of woe,
Which Man deemed old two thousand years ago,
Match me such a marvel save in Eastern clime,
A rose-red city half as old as Time.

John William Burgon,
from "Petra,"
Newdigate Prize poem, 1840

A magnificent adventure

Charles Doughty, one of the most dashing explorers of the 19th century, was a colorful personality and talented writer. He traveled throughout Arabia and the Near East with the nomadic tribes.

We began to descend over a cragged lime-rock, beset with juniper, towards *Wady Mûsa,* Moses' valley, that is Petra, now appearing as a deep cleft very far below us. We saw an encampment of worsted booths, but not of Beduw. These were summering peasants of W. Mûsa: their village is *Eljy* above Petra…

The worthy Burckhardt who in our fathers' time adventuring this way down to Egypt, happily lighted upon the forgotten site of Petra, found these peasants already of a fresh behaviour. He appeared to them as a Syrian stranger and a Moslem, yet hardly they suffered him to pass by the monuments and ascend to sacrifice his lamb upon Mount Hor. Europeans visiting Petra commonly lament the robber violence of these Eljy villagers; but the same were now very good to me…

W. Faraôun we see first, and far off under the sun Kasr Faraôun (Pharaoh's palace): that is the only building in the valley of Petra, and much like a temple, which is of regular masonry. In this country every marvel is ascribed to Pharaoh who made himself, they told me, to be worshipped as a god and here resisted Moses and Aaron.

We have left the limestones with certain rude caverns above; the underlying mountain rocks are ruddy sandstones and pictured often with green-coloured and purple veins: lower in the same are the high cliffs of the hewn monuments. Descending deeply, we came by the principal of them, Greekish, palatial frontispices of two storeys now much decayed by the weather. There is nothing answerable within to the majestical faces, pompous portals leading but into inconsiderable solid halls without ornament; now they are nightstalls of the nomad flocks and blackened with the herdsmen's fires. The valley cliffs, upon both sides, are sculptured in frontispices full of columns and cornices with their inner chambers; the most are of a formal pattern, which I saw later at Medáin Sâlih, and there are other like to those few hewn monuments, which we see in the valley of Jehoshaphat at Jerusalem. A good part of the monuments are manifestly sepulchral, none I can think were houses; and were all numbered together they would not be found very many. The city was surely in the midst and, to judge by that little we see remaining of stone ruins, of clay building. It is thus at Medáin Sâlih: in both towns they might see their monuments standing round about them. We made some chambers in the rock our night's lodging under a little hewn cistern, *Ayn Mûsa,* and which only, of all here seen, I can conjecture to have been a dwelling…

The midday was not here hot, the land-height is perhaps as much as two thousand feet…passing by the hewn theatre we entered the *Sîk;* this is a passage by a deep cleft in the valley head, where are many wild fig trees. Near the mouth is that most perfect of the monuments *Khasna* (treasure-house of) *Faraôun,* whose sculpted columns and cornices are pure lines of a crystalline beauty without blemish, whereupon the golden sun looks from above, and Nature has painted that sand-rock ruddy with iron-rust…

Strange and horrible as a pit, in an inhuman deadness of nature, is this site of the Nabateans' metropolis; the eye

Beduins of the Sinai in a lithograph from Léon de Laborde's influential 1830 book. The fierceness of nomadic Arabs was a popular notion in the 19th-century European imagination, if not always in fact.

recoils from that mountainous close of iron cliffs, in which the ghastly waste monuments of a sumptuous barbaric art are from the first glance an eyesore. The villager, my companion, led me up over the coast to the vast frontispice *ed-Deir:* from these heights above, is a marvellous prospect of the immense low-lying Araba valley and of the sandstone mountain of biblical memory, Mount Hor, rising nigh at our hand; behind us is the high rugged coast of Seir. But the sun setting, we durst not loiter… We hasted through the wild of rocks and blossoming oleanders: many startling rock partridges with loud chuck! chuck! flew up before us and betrayed our lonely footfall. The mule we found where we had left her, in Pharaoh's treasure-house…

Charles M. Doughty,
Travels in Arabia Deserta,
1888

An eye for beauty

Perhaps the greatest foreign writer on the Near East and Arabia since Diodorus of Sicily was the English scholar and soldier called Lawrence of Arabia, who fought there in World War I. A classicist, he knew a good deal about the Nabataeans,

*and his description of Wadi Rum is
particularly moving.*

We were riding for Rumm, the
northern water of the Beni Atiyeh: a
place which stirred my thought, as even
the unsentimental Howeitat had told
me it was lovely…

Day was still young as we rode
between two great pikes of sandstone to
the foot of a long, soft slope poured
down from the domed hills in front of
us. It was tamarisk-covered: the
beginning of the Valley of Rumm, they
said. We looked up on the left to a long
wall of rock, sheering in like a
thousand-foot wave towards the middle
of the valley; whose other arc, to the
right, was an opposing line of steep, red
broken hills. We rode up the slope,
crashing our way through the brittle
undergrowth.

As we went, the brushwood grouped
into thickets whose massed leaves took
on a stronger tint of green the purer for
their contrasted setting in plots of open
sand of a cheerful delicate pink. The
ascent became gentle, till the valley was
a confined tilted plain. The hills on the
right grew taller and sharper, a fair
counterpart of the other side which
straightened itself to one massive
rampart of redness. They drew together
until only two miles divided them: and
then, towering gradually till their
parallel parapets must have been a
thousand feet above us, ran forward in
an avenue for miles.

They were not unbroken walls of
rock, but were built sectionally, in crags
like gigantic buildings, along the two
sides of their street. Deep alleys, fifty
feet across, divided the crags, whose
planes were smoothed by the weather
into huge apses and bays, and enriched

with surface fretting and fracture, like
design. Caverns high up on the
precipice were round like windows:
others near the foot gaped like doors.
Dark stains ran down the shadowed
front for hundreds of feet, like accidents
of use. The cliffs were striated vertically,
in their granular rock: whose main
order stood on two hundred feet of
broken stone deeper in colour and
harder in texture. This plinth did not,
like the sandstone, hang in folds like
cloth but chipped itself into loose courses
of scree, horizontal as the footings of
a wall.

The crags were capped in nests of
domes, less hotly red than the body of
the hill: rather grey and shallow. They
gave the finishing semblance of
Byzantine architecture to this irresistible
place: this processional way greater than
imagination. The Arab armies would
have been lost in the length and
breadth of it, and within the walls a
squadron of aeroplanes could have
wheeled in formation. Our little
caravan grew self-conscious, and fell
dead quiet, afraid and ashamed to
flaunt its smallness in the presence of
the stupendous hills.

Landscapes, in childhood's dream,
were so vast and silent. We looked
backward through our memory for the
prototype up which all men had walked
between such walls toward such an
open square as that in front where this
road seemed to end…

To-day we rode for hours while the
perspectives grew greater and more
magnificent in ordered design, till a gap
in the cliff-face opened on our right to
a new wonder. The gap, perhaps three
hundred yards across, was a crevice in
such a wall; and led to an amphitheater,
oval in shape, shallow in front, and

long-lobed right and left. The walls were precipices, like all the walls of Rumm; but appeared greater, for the pit lay in the very heart of a ruling hill, and its smallness made the besetting heights seem overpowering.

The sun had sunk behind the western wall, leaving the pit in shadow but its dying glare flooded with startling red the wings each side of the entry, and the fiery bulk of the further wall across the great valley. The pit-floor was of damp sand, darkly wooded with shrubs; while about the feet of all the cliffs lay boulders greater than houses, sometimes, indeed, like fortresses which had crashed down from the heights above. In front of us a path, pale with use, zigzagged up the cliff-plinth to the point from which the main face rose, and there it turned precariously southward along a shallow ledge outlined by occasional leafy trees. From between these trees, in hidden crannies of the rock, issued strange cries; the echoes, turned into music, of the voices of the Arabs watering camels at the springs which there flowed out three hundred feet above ground...

To get rid of the dust and strain after my long rides, I went straight up the gully into the face of the hill, along the ruined wall of the conduit by which a spout of water had once run down the ledges to a Nabataean well-house on the valley floor... At the top, the waterfall, el Shellala as the Arabs named it, was only a few yards away.

Its rushing noise came from my left, by a jutting bastion of cliff over whose crimson face trailed long falling runners of green leaves. The path skirted it in an undercut ledge. On the rock-bulge above were clear-cut Nabathaean inscriptions, and a sunk panel incised with a monogram or symbol. Around and about were Arab scratches, including tribe-marks, some of which were witnesses of forgotten migrations...

The people of this stranger-colony were not Greek—at least not in the majority—but Levantines of sorts, aping a Greek culture; and in revenge producing, not the correct banal Hellenism of the exhausted homeland, but a tropical rankness of idea, in which the rhythmical balance of Greek art and Greek ideality blossomed into novel shapes tawdry with the larded passionate colours of the East...

Names rang through my head, each in imagination a superlative: Rum the magnificent, brilliant Petra, Azrak the remote, Batra the very clean.

T. E. Lawrence,
Seven Pillars of Wisdom, 1926

Drawings of bronze imperial coins from "Petra Metropolis" and "Petra Colonia."

Preserving Petra

Petra's ancient Semitic name, Reqem or Raqmu, is said to mean "striped," or "multi-colored," a reference to the extraordinary range of colors of its sandstone. Monuments carved into living rock may seem indestructible, yet the site is threatened by natural erosion and by the neglect of centuries. Today, remedies are being explored to halt this deterioration.

Saving the rose-red city

Petra, the "rose-red" city which is the pride of Jordan, is at risk. Rainwater is attacking its 2,000-year-old classical facades—as is sand, some of it blown by the hoofs of the hundreds of horses on which visitors ride into the city through the Siq—the narrow gorge which forms Petra's main entrance…Today the city is a World Heritage Site, but that designation is scant protection as natural weathering and increasing visitor numbers take their toll.

At present tourists [may] explore hundreds of monuments hewn from cliff faces spread over 26,000 hectares [64,220 acres]—a vast, mountainous, desert panorama. Until the mid-1980s local tribesmen camped in Petra's caves, some reached by a series of stone steps.

Detail of a recent topographic archaeological map of Petra by Leila Nehmé and René Saupin, showing the sector of the Bab el-Siq on the scale of 1:2500. Monuments 34 and 35 are the Obelisk Tomb and the Bab el-Siq Triclinium. Monuments are marked by symbols that reproduce their actual shape as far as possible.

The Government subsequently banished most to modern houses in nearby villages.

In 1989, the Petra National Trust was established in Amman, under the patronage of Queen Noor Al Hussein, to form a network of those "who are committed to a collective international effort to safeguard Petra's unique physical and human heritage."

So now, with the backing of the Jordanian Government, UNESCO [United Nations Educational, Scientific and Cultural Organization] are launching a master plan to protect Petra. Between October and November last year, a multidisciplinary, multinational team of experts researched the vulnerable beauty of this miraculous place... The UNESCO team was coordinated by Michael Barry Lane, a British architect based in Paris as consultant to the cultural heritage division of UNESCO... "We must consider the monuments of Petra in their context because the Nabataeans produced a perfect synthesis with their environment," said Mr Lane. The achievement he most admires was their use of "every drop of water." The hydrological installations, which prevented floods, included miles of channels taking water above mammoth facades and to sculptured drinking fountains, such as the mouth of a vast lion on the route up to the place of sacrifice. They created dams and terraced gardens with amazing sophistication.

The restoration of water systems would allow Petra to flower again. Trees and bushes would be planted on the slopes of the catchment areas to stem erosion and stop the danger of water racing down the Siq, or into the lower levels of excavated monuments. UNESCO will propose the restocking of indigenous animals such as foxes and oryx within a newly defined National Park.

As part of the team, a town planner from Florence University was brought in to look at the "uncontrolled expansion" of villages. Part of the problem stems from rehousing the Bdoul tribe in a new village when they were moved out of Petra's caves. But other local tribes are also encroaching on the city. Another dilemma is the creation of new hotels, which will more than double the 200 available beds within walking distance from Petra. This is not a simple equation because it may prove that explorations over two or three days reduce the crush of day visitors who crowd into Petra in the peak season, and whose movements are at present uncontrolled.

Such issues are being examined by a French sociologist who is based at the Centre for Study and Research on the Contemporary Middle East in Amman. "We propose that local people should become informed guides with formal training," added Mr Lane. They would also become park rangers, and remain in control of visitor access.

Although the narrow Siq will remain the main route into Petra, it will probably be repaved because the original paving was higher than the present level of sand. However, the number of horses available may be reduced from the present 350. Within Petra routes are likely to be waymarked, pointing visitors in the right direction for the Roman amphitheatre, to early burial chambers, and up 500 steps through a ravine to the Sacred Place. Another route yet to be marked winds

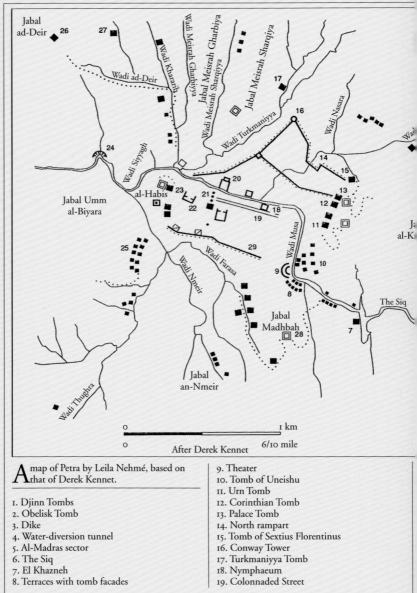

A map of Petra by Leila Nehmé, based on that of Derek Kennet.

1. Djinn Tombs
2. Obelisk Tomb
3. Dike
4. Water-diversion tunnel
5. Al-Madras sector
6. The Siq
7. El Khazneh
8. Terraces with tomb facades
9. Theater
10. Tomb of Uneishu
11. Urn Tomb
12. Corinthian Tomb
13. Palace Tomb
14. North rampart
15. Tomb of Sextius Florentinus
16. Conway Tower
17. Turkmaniyya Tomb
18. Nymphaeum
19. Colonnaded Street

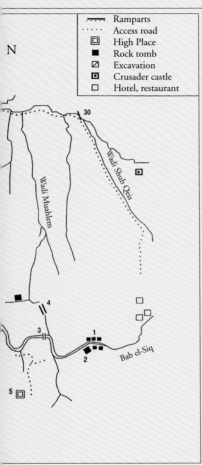

	Ramparts
····	Access road
▣	High Place
■	Rock tomb
▨	Excavation
▣	Crusader castle
☐	Hotel, restaurant

20. Temple of the Winged Lions
21. Triple arch
22. Qasr al-Bint
23. Museum
24. Quarries
25. Summit of Jabal Umm al-Biyara
26. Ad-Deir (the "Monastery")
27. Qattar ad-Deir
28. High Place of Jabal Madhbah
29. South rampart
30. Aqueduct

up past the Lion Triclinium, through timeless gorges where goats meander and bushes cling to crevices, to the largest monument of all—the massive 45-metre-high Ad-Deir, known as the Monastery.

Surprisingly, there is still only a tiny museum to accompany the site. In future a major visitor centre will provide an informative introduction to Petra. It will also offer acceptable souvenirs, instead of the chippings of colourful stone and bottles with camels depicted using coloured sand currently on sale, both of which threaten the city's preservation. Replica and original pottery remain on offer until eventually a ban comes into effect to prevent the sale of the latter.

Only a percentage of Petra is visible, even after decades of excavation...But with the problems of erosion currently eating away at Petra's prime monuments, those still buried may be safest lying undisturbed, while work continues to preserve those already excavated. Pioneer experiments on the waterproofing of sandstone can be tested in the meantime.

Ann Hills,
History Today,
vol. 43, February 1993

How to preserve Petra?

To protect both the constructed monuments of Petra and the natural rock itself is a complex task that has occupied several generations of archaeologists, geologists, and other specialists. One recent study was sponsored by the French electric utility, Electricité de France. Here is an excerpt from the conference report.

I. TO ENSURE WATER CONTROL
In antiquity, Petra, daughter of the

desert, was a lush green oasis. In fact, the Nabataeans had developed an ingenious system for collecting and storing rainwater and drainage water (dams, cisterns), using this water for domestic purposes (fountains), for agricultural needs (irrigation of the gardens of the triclinia), or for cultivation. In doing so, the Nabataeans maintained the level of the groundwater within acceptable limits for the preservation of buildings…

The Nabataean hydraulic system no longer fulfills its function. Rainwater and drainage water seep into the subsoil of Petra, raising the water table. From the effects of heat and evaporation, this salt-bearing water rises by capillary action and permeates the stone of the rock-hewn monuments. After evaporation, the salts crystallize on the surface of the stone and cause deterioration of it. Mechanical or wind erosion then continues the work of destruction…[We have] identified the following goals:
• To combat flooding while restoring Nabataean waterworks and constructing new reservoirs and dams;
• To create underground reservoirs for rain and drainage waters for domestic use;
• To reduce the level of the water table in order to reduce the volume of capillary action, the better to protect monuments;
• To re-create, with the silt of the deposited water, some Nabataean gardens.

2. TO TREAT THE STONE
Having lowered the water table, it will be necessary:
• To reduce the porosity of the stone to continue to restrict capillary action;
• To treat the structure of deteriorated rock in order to strengthen it.

Today, using electrophoresis, it is possible to introduce into the structure of the stone a synthetic mineral (hydroxyapatite) which crystallizes, reinforcing the resistance of the stone to the capillary action of groundwater.

Daniel Brizemeure,
"Comment préserver le site de Petra"
(How to Preserve the Site of Petra),
in the exhibition catalogue
Jordanie: Sur les pas des archéologues
(*Jordan: In the Footsteps of the
Archaeologists*),
Institut du Monde Arabe/SDZ, 1997

Kings of Nabataea

(probable dates)

BC

C. **170–168** Reference to an Aretas (Aretas I) as "*tyrannos* [king] of the Arabs"
C. **120/110–96** Aretas II
96–c. 85/84 Obodas I, son of Aretas II
C. **85/84** Rabbel I
84–62 Aretas III Philhellene, son of Obodas I
62/61–60/59 Obodas II(?)

60–30 Malichus I
30–9 Obodas III
9 BC–AD 40 Aretas IV Lover of His People
40–70 Malichus II, son of Aretas IV, King of Nabataea
70–75/76 Queen Shaqilat II and her son, Rabbel II Life-Giver and Savior of His People, son of Malichus II
75/76–106 Rabbel II Life-Giver and Savior of His People alone

Chronology

BC

C. **10,000–8,000** First traces of Neolithic settlement at Beidha
End 8th–7th century Edomite settlements at Petra
6th(?) century Nabataean nomads filter into Edom
332 Alexander the Great conquers the Near East
312 Greek general Antigonus of Macedonia mounts two expeditions against Petra, with the generals Demetrius (his son) and Athenaeus; both fail
4th–early 2d century Lagids, Ptolemaic kings of Egypt, dominate the region; Nabataeans remain independent; first reference to a Nabataean king, Aretas(?), in the 3d century
259 Papyri of Zeno mention the "people of Rabbel" in the Hauran region of Syria
End 3d–early 2d century Nabataeans extend their territory; they support the Seleucid king Antiochus III (223–187 BC), who drives the Ptolemies from Syria in 202–200 BC
C. **170–168** Reference to a Nabataean King Aretas (Aretas I) as "*tyrannos* [king] of the Arabs"
2d half of 2d century Relations between Nabataeans and their neighbors, the Hasmonaean Jews (Maccabees), turn confrontational
C. **120/110–96** Aretas II is king of Nabataea
100 Hasmonaean king Alexander Jannaeus invades and takes Gaza, which waits in vain for help from the Nabataeans
96–c. 85 Obodas I, son of Aretas II, is king of Nabataea; first dated Nabataean inscription at Petra: "year 1 of Obodas, King of Nabatu"
93–90 Obodas I defeats Jannaeus and takes (or retakes) Moab and Gilead, east of the Jordan River
C. **90–20** Diodorus of Sicily, author of the *Library of History*, with references to the Nabataeans
C. **85/84** Rabbel I is king of Nabataea
85/84 Seleucid king Antiochus XII is defeated and killed by the cavalry of Obodas I, who is deified and probably buried at Eboda (Avdat), in the Negev
84–62 Aretas III Philhellene, son of Obodas I, is king of Nabataea

84–72/71 Aretas III reigns in Damascus
C. **82** Aretas III defeats Hasmonaean king Alexander Jannaeus, who soon reconquers territory in southern Syria, east of the Jordan River and toward Gaza
67 Aretas III allies with Hyrcanus II, eldest son of Jannaeus (dethroned by his brother Aristobulus), and welcomes him to Petra
65–64 Aretas III helps Hyrcanus II besiege Jerusalem, but the Romans defeat them in the Jordan River valley
64–63 Pompey the Great, Roman general, creates the Roman province of Syria and takes Jerusalem
C. **64/63 BC–after AD 23** Strabo, author of the *Geography*, with references to the Nabataeans
62 Marcus Aemilius Scaurus, Roman governor, leads an expedition against Petra; although it largely fails, Aretas III becomes a client of Rome, paying an indemnity
C. **62/61–60/59** Obodas II is king of Nabataea(?); uncertain reign known only through inscriptions and coins
60–30 Malichus I is king of Nabataea
55 Aulus Gabinius, Roman governor of Syria, leads an attack against "the city of the Nabataeans"
47 Malichus I sends cavalry to the aid of Julius Caesar in Alexandria
40 Malichus I supports the Parthian invasion of Syria-Palestine, which fails; he is subject to a heavy fine, including part of the Arabian territory of Nabataea and revenues from the Dead Sea bitumen industry (these are given by Antony to Cleopatra in 34 BC)
31 Rivalry between the Roman generals Antony and Octavian (later Augustus Caesar); Malichus hesitates in his allegiance; following the victory of Octavian at the battle of Actium, he tries to form an alliance with him, betraying Cleopatra; Herod I, the Great, king of Judaea, defeats a Nabataean army, near Philadelphia-Amman
30–9 Obodas III is king of Nabataea
30 Nabataeans purchase the territory of Auranitis (the Hauran), which they control until 23 BC

27 Octavian becomes Augustus; beginning of the Roman Empire; Nabataea is not included in the imperial province of Syria

25–24 Expedition of Aelius Gallus, prefect of Egypt, into Arabia Felix includes a Nabataean contingent, but according to Strabo, it fails, owing to the plots of Obodas's minister, Syllaeus; Red Sea commerce is diverted to Egypt, affecting Nabataean caravan trade

9–8 Intrigues of Syllaeus with Herod and the Romans; Aretas IV, who is not Obodas's son, takes power at Petra; Augustus eventually recognizes him

9 BC–AD 40 Aretas IV Lover of His People is king of Nabataea; his wives are Huldu (9/8 BC–AD 15/16) and Shaqilat (AD 16 or 18–40)

4 Death of Herod I of Judaea; the Nabataeans take part in the subsequent repression of revolts; his kingdom is divided among his three sons

C. 4 Birth of Christ

AD

C. 27 Herod Antipas, son of Herod I, divorces his wife, daughter of Aretas, who invades the Golan and Hauran, the Syrian possessions of Herod Philippus, another son of Herod, and defeats Antipas (before 34)

37 Herod Agrippa I, grandson of Herod I, reforms and expands Judaean kingdom and passes it to his son Herod Agrippa II in 44

40–70 Malichus II, son of Aretas IV, King of Nabataea rules; his wife is Shaqilat II

66–67 Start of the Jewish revolt against Rome; Herod Agrippa II and Malichus II support the Romans

70–106 Rabbel II Life-Giver and Savior of His People, son of Malichus II, is king of Nabataea; last independent king before Roman annexation

70–75/76 Queen mother, Shaqilat II, is regent

76–102 Rabbel II wedded to Gamilat

C. 76 Last Nabataean epitaphs at Hegra

C. 92–96 Death of Herod Agrippa II, whose kingdom is incorporated into the Roman province of Syria

102–106 Reign of Hagru, second queen; Bosra becomes the second capital of the kingdom

106 Roman emperor Trajan annexes Nabataea (apparently without force; possibly upon the death of Rabbel II) and creates the Province of Arabia, with Bosra as capital; Petra receives the honorific title of Metropolis

111–114 Construction of the Via Nova Traiana, a road that establishes a link from Bosra to Aqaba, passing near Petra

127–130 Titus Aninius Sextius Florentinus is Roman governor of Arabia; he probably died in Petra and is buried there

130/131 Emperor Hadrian visits Petra, which takes the title Petra, Hadrianic Metropolis

218–222 Under the reign of Emperor Elagabalus, Petra becomes a Roman colony, Petra Colonia

C. 295–314 In the administrative reorganization undertaken by Emperor Diocletian, Petra may be a part of a new Province of Arabia, within the Provincia Palaestina Salutaris

C. 304 Persecution of Christians in Petra, under the prefect Maximus

343 First mention of a Christian bishop "from Arabia"

May 19, 363 Earthquake destroys much of Petra, including the Colonnaded Street

C. 400 The province takes the name Palaestina Tertia

419 Earthquake again gravely damages Petra

C. 423 Forced Christian conversions in Petra, during Bar Sauma episode

July 24, 446 Former Urn Tomb is dedicated as a Christian church

451–535 Territory of Palaestina Tertia is extended further to the north

528–582 Dates of an archive of papyri found in a church at Petra in 1993

July 9, 551 Earthquake destroys Petra

630–638 Muslim conquest of the region, probably including Petra

661 Mu'āwiyah I becomes first Ummayad dynasty ruler of the Muslim Empire of the Caliphate, whose capital is Damascus

747 Earthquake again damages Petra

750 Abbasid dynasty overthrows the Ummayads; capital of the caliphate transferred to Baghdad

1114–16(?) Baldwin I and later Frankish Crusader kings of Jerusalem construct fortresses in "Oultre Jourdain"; at Petra, these include al-Wu'eira castle in Li Vaux Moise (Wadi Musa), and the fort of al-Habis on a high point above the city

1187–89 Salah ad-Din (Saladin) defeats the Franks at Hattin and Karak and occupies the Petra fortresses

1217 Thetmar, a German pilgrim, passes near Petra and mentions it in his chronicle

1276 Mamluk Sultan Baybars I, traveling from Cairo, sees Petra. His chronicler, Numeiri (1279–1332), later records a description drawn from the work of the annalist Ibn 'Abd ez-Zaher

August 22, 1812 Johann Ludwig Burckhardt rediscovers Petra

Further Reading

THE TRAVELERS

Burckhardt, J. L., *Travels in Syria and the Holy Land*, 1822

Doughty, C., *Travels in Arabia Deserta*, 1888

Irby, C. L., and J. Mangles, *Travels in Egypt and Nubia, Syria, and Asia Minor during the Years 1817 and 1818*, 1823

Laborde, L. de, *Voyage de l'Arabie Pétrée, par Léon de Laborde et Linant*, 1830–33 (English ed., *Journey through Arabia Petraea*, 1836)

Luynes, H. d'Albert, duc de, *Voyage d'exploration à la Mer Morte, à Pétra et sur la rive gauche du Jourdain*, 1871–76

Roberts, D., *Egypt, Syria, and the Holy Land*, 1842–49

Robinson, E., *Biblical Researches in Palestine and the Adjacent Regions*, 1856, 1867

CLASSIC WORKS

Bachmann, W., C. Watzinger, and T. Wiegand, *Petra: Wissenschaftliche Veröffentlichungen des deutsch-türkischen Denkmalschutz-Kommandos*, 1921

Brünnow, R. E., and A. von Domaszewski, *Die Provincia Arabia*, 1904–9

Cantineau, J., *Le Nabatéen*, 1930, 1932

Dalman, G., *Petra und seine Felsheiligtümer*, 1908

———, *Neue Petra-Forschungen und der heilige Felsen von Jerusalem*, 1912

Jaussen, J., and R. Savignac, *Mission archéologique en Arabie*, 1909, 1914

Kammerer, A., *Pétra et la Nabatène*, 1929–30

Kennedy, A. B. W., *Petra: Its History and Monuments*, 1925

Murray, M. A., *Petra: The Rock City of Edom*, 1939

Musil, A., *Arabia Petraea*, vol. 2, 1907

Woolley, L., and T. E. Lawrence, *The Wilderness of Zin*, 1936

RECENT ARCHAEO-
LOGICAL STUDIES,
ILLUSTRATED BOOKS,
GUIDES, AND NOVELS

Amadasi Guzzo, M. G., and E. Equini Schneider, *Petra*, 1997, 1998

Bowersock, G. W., *Roman Arabia*, 1983

Browning: I., *Petra*, 1973, 1982, 1989

Burton, R. F., *The Land of Midian (Revisited)*, 1984

Cardinal, P., ed., *Pétra: Le Dit des pierres*, 1993

Dentzer, J.-M., and F. Zayadine, "L'Espace urbain de Pétra," in *Studies in the History of Archaeology of Jordan*, vol. 4, 1992

———, "Pétra, le refuge des nomades," in *Sciences et avenir*, 1991

Fedden, R., and J. Thomson, *Crusader Castles*, 1957

Glueck, N., *Deities and Dolphins: The Story of the Nabataeans*, 1965

Graf, D. F., ed., *Rome and the Arabian Frontier: From the Nabataeans to the Saracens (Collected Studies, Cs594)*, 1998

Hammond, P. C., "A City and a People—Lost and Found," *Ancient History Bulletin* 11:2–3, 1997

———, "The Excavation of Petra: Cultural Aspects of Nabataean Architecture, Religion, Art, and Influence," in *Studies in the History and Archaeology of Jordan*, vol. 1, 1982

———, *The Nabataeans—Their History, Culture and Archaeology*, 1973

———, *The Temple of the Winged Lions, Petra, Jordan, 1973–1990*, 1996

Harding, G. L., *The Antiquities of Jordan*, 1959, 1967, 1974

Joukowsky, M. S., ed., *Petra Great Temple*, vol. 1, *Brown University Excavations, 1993–1997*, 1998

Khouri, R. G., *Petra: A Guide to the Capital of the Kingdom of the Nabataeans*, 1986

———, *Petra: A Brief Guide to the Antiquities*, 1988

Linder, M., ed., *Petra und das Königreich der Nabatäer*, 1970, 1989

———, ed., *Petra: Neue Ausgrabungen und Entdeckungen*, 1986

McKenzie, J. S., "The Dating of the Principal Monuments at Petra: A New Approach," in *Studies in the Archaeology and History of Jordan*, vol. 3, 1987

———, "The Development of the Nabataean Sculpture at Petra and Tannur," in *Palestine Exploration Quarterly*, no. 120, 1988

———, *The Architecture of Petra*, 1990

The Nabataeans, publication of the First International Conference of Aram, *Aram Periodical*, no. 2, 1990

Nehmé, L., "L'Espace cultuel de Pétra à l'époque nabatéene," in *Topoi Orient-Occident* 7:2, 1997

Nehmé, L., and F. Villeneuve, *Pétra: Métropole de l'Arabie antique*, 1999

Nehmé, L., and R. Saupin, *Atlas archéologique de Pétra*, forthcoming

Parr, P. J., "Sixty Years of Excavation in Petra. A Critical Assessment," in *Aram Periodical*, no. 2, 1990

Patrich, J., *The Formation of Nabatean Art*, 1990

Petra-Ez Zantur I: Ergibnisse der Schweizerisch-Liechtensteinischen Ausgrabungen, 1988–1992, 1996

Runciman, S., *A History of the Crusades*, 3 vols., 1951–54

Spectrum Guide to Jordan, 1999

Starcky, J., "Pétra et la Nabatène," in *Supplément au Dictionnaire de la Bible*, vol. 7, 1966

Taylor, J., *Petra*, 1993, 1995

Tholbecq, L., "Les Sanctuaires des Nabatéens: État de la question…," in *Topoi Orient-Occident* 7:2, 1997

Weber, T., and R. Wenning, eds., *Petra: Antike Felsstadt zwischen arabischer Tradition und griechischer Norm*, 1997

Wenning, R., *Die Nabatäer: Denkmäler und Geschichte*, 1997

Zayadine, F., "L'Espace urbain du grand Pétra: Les routes et les stations caravanières," in *Annual of the Department of Antiquities of Jordan*, vol. 36, 1992

———, ed., *Petra and the Caravan Cities*, 1990

Zayadine, F., and S. Farajat, "The Petra National Trust Site Projects: Excavation and Clearance at Petra and Beidha," *Annual of the Department of Antiquities of Jordan*, vol. 35, 1991

PERIODICALS AND SERIES

Annual of the Department of Antiquities of Jordan (ADAJ), Amman

Studies in the History and Archaeology of Jordan (SHAJ), Amman (proceedings of the International Conferences on the History and Archaeology of Jordan)

List of Illustrations

Index

Acknowledgments

The authors warmly thank all those who gave their kind assistance: in the Near East, Dr. Ghazi Bisheh, Dr. Fawzi Zayadine, Khairiye Amr, Sulaiman Farajat, Mohamed al-Shaubaki, and their colleagues in the Jordanian Department of Antiquities; Zeidoun al-Moheisen and Dominique Tarrier; Geneviève Jean-Van Rossum, Agnès Romatet, the Cultural Service and Embassy of France; Jean-Pierre Braun, Laurent Tholbecq, Ina Kehrberg, Pierre-Marie Blanc, Gabriel Humbert, François Bernel and their colleagues at the IFAPO, Fathers Jean-Baptiste Humbert and Jean-Michel de Tarragon (Ecole Biblique et Archéologique Française); Artemis and Martha Joukowsky and the American Mission of the Great Temple; Pierre Bikai and ACOR; Jane Taylor, Thomas Weber, de Mayence, Bernhard Kolb, and the Archeological Seminar of the University of Basel. In France: the members of the "Syrie du Sud-Pétra" team of the CNRS, especially Roland Bierry, Frank Braemer, Jean-François Breton, Jacques Leblanc, Leila Nehmé, Jean Sapin, René Saupin, Estelle and François Villeneuve; Geneviève Dollfus, Pascale and Xavier Linant de Bellefonds, Maurice Sartre, Jacques Seigne; Father Jacques Briend (Musée Biblique), Dominique Gerin (Cabinet des Médailles at the Bibliothèque Nationale de France), Philippe Cardinal (IMA), the scientific patronage of the EDF and the Laboratoire Valectra, the photographer Sylvain Pelly, the Magnum agency, and René Burri.

Photograph Credits

Text Credits

Daniel Brizemeure, in *Jordanie: Sur les pas des archéologues,* Institut du Monde Arabe/SDZ, 1997; Iain Browning, *Petra,* 1973, courtesy of Chatto & Windus; Philippe Cardinal, ed., *Le Dit des pierres,* Actes Sud, 1993; excerpt from "The Pendulum of Fortune," from *Deities and Dolphins* by Nelson Glueck. Copyright renewed 1993 by Dr. Helen Iglauer Glueck. Reprinted by permission of Farrar, Straus & Giroux, LLC; Ann Hills, in *History Today,* February 1993; Sir Alexander B. W. Kennedy, *Petra: Its History and Monuments,* London: Country Life, 1925; from *Seven Pillars of Wisdom* by T. E. Lawrence, by permission of the Trustees of the Seven Pillars of Wisdom Trust; Maurice Sartre, *Inscriptions de la Jordanie,* vols. 4, 21, Librairie Paul Geuthner, Paris, 1993; *Petra,* 1993 © Jane Taylor, by Permission of Aurum Press, London; Fawzi Zayadine, in *Les Dossiers d'archéologie,* no. 163, September 1991.

Jean-Marie Dentzer is Director of the Institut Français d'Archéologie du
Proche-Orient and a professor at the Université de Paris I. He is past leader of an archaeological
team from the Centre National de la Recherche Scientifique (CNRS), working in southern
Syria and Jordan, and author of numerous specialized works, including the *Hauran* series.
His articles have appeared in *Syrie: Le Monde de la Bible*, and *Les Dossiers d'archéologie*.

Christian Augé is Director of Research at the Centre National de la Recherche Scientifique
(CNRS). A specialist in ancient coins and the classical iconography
of the Near East, he succeeded Jean-Marie Dentzer as leader of an archaeological
team in southern Syria and the Petra region of Jordan. He has collaborated on numerous
publications on the ancient period of the region and also studies
the modern Near East.

To Jacqueline, Paul, and Jacques.
To Hélène, Jean-Christophe, and Ariane.

Translated from the French by Laurel Hirsch; some documents
translated by David Baker

First published in the United Kingdom in 2000 by Thames & Hudson Ltd,
181A High Holborn, London WC1V 7QX

Reprinted 2006, 2009, 2010, 2016

English translation © 2000 Harry N. Abrams, Inc., New York

Copyright © 1999 Gallimard

British Library Cataloguing-in-Publication Data

A catalogue record for this book is available from the British Library

ISBN 978-0-500-30099-2

Printed and bound in China

To find out about all our publications, please
visit **www.thamesandhudson.com**. There you
can subscribe to our e-newsletter, browse or download
our current catalogue, and buy any titles that are in print.